It Works for Me with Critical Thinking

A Step-by-Step Guide

By Charlie Sweet, Hal Blythe,
& Russell Carpenter

NEW FORUMS PRESS INC.

Published in the United States of America
by New Forums Press, Inc.1018 S. Lewis St.
Stillwater, OK 74074
www.newforums.com

Copyright © 2019 by New Forums Press, Inc.

All rights reserved. No part of this publication may be reproduced or transmitted in any form or by any means, electronic or mechanical, including photocopy, or any information storage or retrieval system, without permission in writing from the publisher.

Library of Congress Cataloging-in-Publication Data Pending

This book may be ordered in bulk quantities at discount from New Forums Press, Inc., P.O. Box 876, Stillwater, OK 74076 [Federal I.D. No. 73 1123239]. Printed in the United States of America.

ISBN 10: 1-58107-336-4
ISBN 13: 978-1-58107-336-2

Table of Contents

Preface v

I. Introduction to Critical Thinking 1

II. Approaches: An Overview...7
    Uncertainty as a Vehicle for Critical Thinking 8
    Using Wikis to Foster and Create Student Accountability for Learning 11
    Creating a Critical Thinking Mindset: Using Self-Reflective Teaching
        Questions/Directives to Enhance Learning 13
    Group Quizzes Encourage Critical Thinking, Team-Building,
        and Improved Understanding 15
    Five-Step Process for Teaching Critical Thinking..17
    Edward de Bono's Six Thinking Hats, an Instructional Method
        to Teach Critical Thinking 19
    Increasing Critical Thinking Skills and Course Success
        through Co-requisite Courses 21
    Modifying Project-Based Learning Concepts for Laboratory Settings 23
    Applying Critical Thinking within Administrative Contexts:
        Perspectives from Two Programs 25

III. Strategies: An Overview 31
    Advocacy-Inspired Critical-Thinking Practices 32
    Fostering Critical Thinking through Diversity 33
    Classroom Debates: The Good, The Bad, and The Anxiety-Provoking 36
    Using a Relic of Past Pedagogical Practices to Enhance Critical
        Thinking in 21st Century Classrooms 38
    Applying Visualization Techniques to Literacy Instruction 41
    Group Work as a Tool to Enhance Critical Thinking 43
    Do Reflection Papers Facilitate Critical Thinking?..46
    Making It Relevant: Building Online Discussions 47
    What Flavor Are Your Questions?...49
    Engaging Critical Thinking in Online Discussions 51

 Cracking Open the Books: Reading to Foster Critical Thinking 53
 Think about It!—Facilitating Student Thinking
   with Reflective Responses 56
 Understanding Ethos in the Public Speaking Classroom 58
 Let's Have a Discussion 61
 If You Can Teach It, You Probably Are Thinking Critically About It 62
 Embracing the Dark Side: Role-Playing the Bad Guy
   in an Education Environment 64

IV. Assignments and Exercises: An Overview 67
 Technology to Enhance Preservice Teachers' Critical Thinking 68
 To Write Dirty, You Have to Know What Clean Is 70
 Extending the Thinking of Preservice Early Childhood Educators
   through Creative Application 73
 Classroom Mobiling: A Critical Thinking Exercise for the
   Millennial Student 75
 Using Students' Career Dreams to Think and Research
   Outside the Box 78
 Constructing Images and Essential Questions that Critically
   Respond to a Theme 82
 Finding Relevancy in the News 84
 Relating Readers' Experiences to Themes from an Assigned Textbook 86
 Inquiry-Based Problem Solving via Online Discussion Boards 89
 Debating as Critical Thinking 91
 Role Plays: Sometimes Awkward, But Very Often Effective 92
 Building Students' Critical Thinking Skills in One Minute: Effort
   and Engagement Questions 94
 Interactive Participatory Class Activities that Stimulate Critical Thinking 97
 Forcing Students to Make an Informed Choice 99
 An Effective Practical Tip for Critical Thinking 102
 Each One Write One 104

Afterword 107

About the Authors 109

Preface

Recently, the local newspaper interviewed one of the speakers in the University's Chautauqua Lecture Series, Cornell University Professor of Economics Robert Frank. When Frank was asked, "What's your elevator pitch for higher education?" he offered an explanation that underscored the significance of critical thinking:

> When you meet somebody who's well trained in critical thinking, it's immediately apparent to you. We're living in a world now where people can doctor photographs. They can shout fake news. They can spin a conspiracy theory. If you're not equipped to think skeptically about the arguments people make to you, then you're ever more at risk in the environment we inhabit now. (p. 4C)

For over a decade we have served on the Faculty Development Workgroup (now the Teaching & Learning Workgroup) of the Commonwealth's Council on Postsecondary Education. In discussions with our colleagues on the committee, we have realized that schools other than our university, such as the University of Louisville and University of the Cumberlands, also have had Quality Enhancement Programs (QEP) devoted to critical thinking. We didn't really consult with each other to create the QEPs, but we have collaborated by sharing the costs of speakers as well as putting on workshops for each other.

Moreover, in selecting proposals for the state's teaching and learning conference, the Pedagogicon, and editing issues of the *Journal of Faculty Development*, we have run across a spate of pieces on critical thinking. Also, last year for our online professional development system, DEEP (Developing Excellence in Eastern's Professors), we created an entire course centered on Critical and Creative Thinking.

Our point is that critical thinking has become the central topic of many higher education conversations. And just as Elvis pushed for "a little less conversation, a little more action," so has academia. The purpose of this book is to provide a venue for that action, to allow our colleagues from across the country to share what works for them.

Simply put, the academy must become better at instilling critical thinking so that for graduates it becomes a habit of mind.

In this book, the twelfth in our "It Works for Me Series," you will find the selections are more evidence-based and focused than when we began twenty years ago, and our contributors seem to be applying more critical thinking to their own writing.

Reference

Martin, T. (2018, April 23). Making the case for investing more public dollars in higher education. *The Lexington Herald-Leader*, 1C-4C.

I. Introduction to Critical Thinking

Have you ever heard of the Indian parable about the three blindfolded men who are asked to place a hand on a beast in order to judge its identity? Each man touches a different part of the animal—the tusk, the hide, and the tail—and each offers a different guess as to the type of beast in question. As a result of sampling different parts, the three cannot agree on the identity of the beast before them.

Critical thinking is much like the Indian beast. Everybody comes at it from a different direction, and each discipline seems to offer its own definition. While, to use another metaphor, critical thinking isn't exactly the Tower of Babel, it is close enough so as to sow seeds of confusion in those who seek to have an honest discussion about its nature.

And, make no mistake, critical thinking is an important concept in education at any level, especially higher education. Derek Bok, the former president of Harvard, observes in *Our Underachieving Colleges* (2006) that "it is impressive to find faculty members agreeing almost unanimously that teaching students to think critically is the principal aim of undergraduate education" (p. 109). The American Association of University Professors asserts that "critical thinking . . . is the hallmark of American education—an education designed to create thinking citizens for a free society."

Unfortunately, the rough beast of critical thinking has already slouched its way into academia. According to Arum and Roksa's *Academically Adrift* (2011), the lack of rigor in higher ed classes has produced graduates who can't write well, solve complex problems, or think critically: "three semesters of college education thus have a barely noticeable impact on students' skills in critical thinking, complex reasoning, and writing" (p. 35). Carr in *The Shallows* (2010) reports that between 1998 and 2008 "critical reading scores fell 3.3%" (p. 146). And since Arum and Roksa's research, the situation has worsened: millennial students have been replaced by the iGens, those students born in 1995 or later, whose critical thinking deficiency is evident when they perform research and look for evidence. Because they read so little and spend almost seven hour per day online, Twenge (2017) comments, "iGen'ers need to be taught about sources and evaluating evidence . . . [ellipsis ours] this type of critical thinking needs to be emphasized through iGen`ers` education and within specific areas" (p. 208). In short, for an iGen student, a blog (though it might be merely the opinions of a sixth-grader) is equally evidence-based as an article in *Science*. Rosen (2010) arrives at a similar conclusion: "So it appears that even college students lack the necessary skills to critically analyze information they find on the Internet, and they believe that all information is about equally truthful and has the same value" (p. 156).

While many factors contribute to the lack of critical thinking in academia, we're focusing on one major problem at the beginning of this book—the lack of a consistent definition of critical thinking that can be applied across the disciplines. Bok, for instance, offers his definition of the "ability to think critically" as a five-step process:

- "to ask pertinent questions,
- [to] recognize and define problems,
- [to] identify the arguments on all sides of an issue,
- [to] search for and use relevant data, and
- [to] arrive in the end at carefully reasoned judgments." (p. 109)

Brookfield (1990) describes a "critically alert, questioning cast of mind" as one that "entails a readiness to scrutinize claims of universal truth with skepticism, to reject monocausal explanations of complex issues, and to mistrust final solutions to intractable problems" (p. 24). In *Learning to Think Things Through* (2009), Gerry Nosich divides critical thinking into a three-part process:

- "critical thinking involves asking questions."
- "critical thinking involves trying to answer those questions by reasoning them out."
- "critical thinking involves believing the results of our reasoning." (pp. 5-6)

One of the most comprehensive and specific definitions of critical thinking is provided by the Foundation for Critical Thinking. Its founders, Richard Paul and Linda Elder, have written a series of books on the subject that breaks critical thinking into three specific components of fair-minded critical thinkers:

I. Intellectual Character (8 traits)
- Intellectual integrity
- Intellectual humility
- Confidence in reason
- Intellectual perseverance
- Fairmindedness
- Intellectual courage
- Intellectual empathy

- Intellectual independence. (*Guide to Critical Thinking*, 2009, p. 7)

II. Intellectual Standards (9 traits)
- Clarity
- Accuracy
- Precision
- Relevance
- Depth
- Breadth
- Logic
- Significance
- Fairness. (*Guide to Critical Thinking*, 2009, p. 16)

III. Parts of Thinking/Elements of Thought (8 parts)
- Purpose
- Questions
- Information
- Inferences
- Concepts
- Assumptions
- Implications and Consequences
- Points of View. (*Guide to Critical Thinking*, 2009, p. 20)

Unfortunately, for our first Quality Enhancement Plan (QEP), our University adopted the Paul and Elder model. Yes, their model is quite extensive, but picture students walking into any classroom on campus and finding three posters with the 25 traits intimidatingly staring down at them. As our Teaching & Learning Center bore responsibility for teaching the critical thinking trainers—QEP Coaches—we sought a way to make the transmission of knowledge easier. As we explain on p. 67 of *Transforming Your Students into Deep Learners: A Guide for Instructors* (2016), we applied what Nosich in *Learning to Think Things Through* (2009) called a fundamental and powerful concept, "one that can be used to explain or think out a huge body of questions, problems, information, and situations" (p. 105). In our case, we simplified and synthesized the "huge" body of 25 traits into our six standards of deep critical thinking.

Using Anderson and Krathwohl's Bloom's Revised Taxonomy (2001), we identified critical thinking with the higher order skill of **Evaluating** for our definition of critical thinking as **evaluating the argument**. Our distillation of the basic traits was formulated into the acronym **PASSOR** in order to provide a simple mnemonic device for recalling them. So to evaluate an argument (and in our rhetoric classes we learned that everything's an argument), we examine the argument through these six lenses:

- **Perspective**: Collect and analyze all claims and counter claims. Prepare to argue the issue from at least two sides—i.e., question all assumptions.
- **Accuracy**: Check your facts. Newspaper often use two separate sources for verification, but in this era of fake news, finding three independent sources—triangulation—is a better way to go.
- **Sufficiency**: Enough details must be supplied to support any claims, and these details must take into account the complexity of the claim
- **Specificity**: Return to the world of journalism, and make certain to examine the 4 Ws of Who, What, Where, and When. What are the credentials of the who making the claim? What does the argument actually claim? Is the supporting evidence recent, or has it been superseded? What is the true source of the claim, the evidence?
- **Objectivity**: Take personal biases into account, especially those of a political nature. Have all points of view been included?
- **Relevance**: The evidence must align with the claim. Make certain that the evidence has a direct relationship to the claim.

Perhaps our definition of critical thinking and its reduction to the super six standards of PASSOR only complicates matters, especially in your field. We are also aware that different fields will offer different definitions. In fact, a professor friend of ours in chemistry recently told us that critical thinking is the new scientific method. Maybe someday our collective blindness will be replaced by a singular comprehensive definition that this book helps create.

We encourage you to use this book either to determine or to construct the meaning of critical thinking in your field. The writers herein have provided a breadth and depth of information that will surely help you come to terms with that rough beast of critical thinking. As usual, organizing these tips provided a critical thinking challenge of its own. We began sorting by the subjects of the tips, finding that about 15% dealt with reflecting and revising and another 15% focused on researching. As the remaining 70% were concerned with singular topics, we finally opted for a broader organizational scheme that ran from theory to practice, from the most general essays to very specific exercises.

References

Anderson, L., & Krathwohl, D. (2012). *A taxonomy for learning, teaching, and assessing: A revision of Bloom's taxonomy of educational objectives.* New York, NY: Longman.

Arum, R. & Roksa, J. (2011). *Academically adrift: Limited learning on college campuses*. Chicago, IL: University of Chicago Press.

Bok, D. (2006). *Our underachieving colleges*. Princeton, NJ: Princeton University Press.

Brookfield, S. (1990). *The skillful teacher*. San Francisco: CA: Jossey-Bass.

Carr, N. (2010). *The shallows*. New York: NY: W. W. Norton.

Elder, L. & Paul, R. (2009). *Guide to critical thinking*. Dillon Beach, CA: Foundation for Critical Thinking.

Nosich, G. (2009). *Learning to think things through* (3rd ed). Upper Saddle River, NJ: Pearson Prentice Hall.

Rosen, L. (2010). *Rewired*. New York, NY: Palgrave MacMillan.

Scott, J. (2005, 9 Nov.). Statement on behalf of AAUP, as part of testimony before the Pennsylvania General Assembly's House Select Committee on Student Academic Freedom. Retrieved from http://www.aaup.org/AAUP/GR/Academic+Bill+of+Rights+State+Level/Scotttestimony.htm

Sweet, C., Blythe, H., Phillips, B., & Carpenter, R. (2016). *Transforming your students into deep learners: A guide for instructors*. Stillwater, OK: New Forums Press.

Twenge, J. (2017). *iGen: Why today's super-connected kids are growing up less rebellious, more tolerant, less happy—and completely unprepared for childhood*. New York, NY: Atria Books.

II. Approaches: An Overview

The following section contains eight approaches to critical thinking—general, more theoretical methods of considering the best ways of implementing critical thinking in your classroom. Most of us have our own traditional ways of regarding this problem, so take note the variety of approaches the writers suggest: uncertainty, wikis, creating the needed mindset, quizzes, a five-step process, the six thinking hats, co-requisite courses, and project-based learning concepts. Truthfully, our goal is to nudge you out of your comfort zone so you will try approaches new to you.

When you have finished, we challenge and encourage you to choose at least one new approach, and experiment with it in one of your courses, if only for a short while. Small changes can often yield big results.

Uncertainty as a Vehicle for Critical Thinking

Building around adult stages of development that were initially framed in 1970 by Perry (1998) and later refined by Baxter Magolda (1992), Craig Nelson (2003) applied the concepts as modes of thinking relevant to teaching. Within the stages framework, Nelson suggests that the transition from one stage to another constitutes critical thinking in a broad sense. In particular, Nelson indicates that the transition from the lowest-level stage of Absolute/Dualistic knowing to the next stage in which knowledge is viewed in a more nuanced fashion involves understanding knowledge as uncertain. With Nelson's notion of critical thinking in hand, I have incorporated a variety of aspects of knowledge uncertainty into my courses. In addition to using these elements of uncertainty in mathematics courses, I have also used them in a first-year seminar course about "ways of knowing" and in faculty development activities.

In this regard, I have found it helpful to explore the following questions as I develop and implement courses:

- Is there an *element of uncertainty* in my course that students will see or experience?
- Is there an activity that would help my students "rethink their assumptions, and examine their mental models of reality" (Bain, 2004)?

As I identify ways to answer the above questions, I have been drawn to (among other things) threshold concepts. According to Pinter (2017), a Threshold Concept is like a portal, opening up a new and previously inaccessible way of thinking about something. Comprehending a threshold concept may lead to a transformed internal frame for subject matter, subject landscape, or even world view.

The short video *A Private Universe* (1987) offers some misconceptions about basic astronomy ideas; the video has helped me invite students into consideration of preconceptions and misconceptions. I want to ask myself: what are some student preconceptions or misconceptions that I can attempt to address within my course? Leski (2015) offers a way of connecting preconceptions to creativity that has fueled my imagination:

> Unlearning is about questioning what you thought you knew. ... Preconceptions hinder creativity. Creativity involves preventing yourself from making what you already "know." Creativity involves thwarting your own preconceived plans, abilities, and assumptions. Unlearning allows for a fresh perspective.

I have discovered that I find it important to address some preconceptions in my mathematics classroom quickly and directly; for example, I immediately address (through classroom activities and commentary) the misguided notion that "to be good at mathematics, you must be able to calculate quickly." In contrast, for a preconception such as "I'm simply not good at mathematical problem-solving," I approach students more obliquely and gradually by encouraging a growth mindset (Dweck, 2007).

Another fruitful question that I consider for each course I teach is some version of: what topic(s) do my students often encounter with a very limited initial understanding for which some uncertainty might invite interest in effective critical thinking? For example, in a general education mathematics course the students are both confronted and enlightened by exploring the difference between one billion and one trillion. I draw a number line with 0 at the left end and 1 trillion at the right end; I then invite a few students to locate where 1 billion occurs on the number line (answer: very, very close to 0 since 1 billion is only $1/1000^{th}$ of 1 trillion). Because we deal in the course with many problems that have solutions that are very large numbers, this exercise invites students to do more than simply calculate answers.

In a similar vein, when students are confronted with current or fundamental knowledge limitations in mathematics, they are forced to engage in critical thinking as they attempt to make some sense of approaching problems in ways that are other than a dualistic black/white or right/wrong. Examples of topics that I include directly or that I reference include computer processing speed, The Uncertainty Principle in physics, Gödel's Incompleteness Theorem in symbolic logic, mathematical chaos, and Arrow's Impossibility Theorem in regard to ranked voting schemes. Over years of teaching, I have trained myself to seek out examples by asking: What are some important concepts or ideas for which I want students to understand limitations of our knowledge?

Another interesting and fruitful question for me in developing a course is: Are there good examples that "surprise" students with an outcome and thus lead to deeper learning opportunities via critical thinking? What will work as "counterintuitive" depends on the specific course. I have discovered a variety of topics that readily lead to counterintuitive outcomes that in turn invite critical exploration. Examples that I routinely employ include different ranked voting methods leading to different winners, the flaw in combining averages, and mathematics problems that have multiple correct answers.

As a means of helping my students grapple with the significance of knowledge uncertainty in mathematics, I sometimes include the following prompt for their response as a take-home exam question:

> There are several places (concepts or problems) during the course where we have encountered uncertainties or impossibilities within mathematics. Comment on ***at least four*** such problems or concepts and include what we seem to know and what limita-

tions are encountered. What do you see as implications, broadly speaking, that follow from the limitations of mathematics?

Their responses to the prompt have helped me to better understand how to refine my uses of uncertainty in the development of my courses.

In addition to students developing some effective critical thinking skills by their exploration of knowledge uncertainty, I have discovered that teaching is more interesting and fun with uncertainty intentionally in the mix. The teaching and learning atmosphere feels more real and vibrant to me. In the words of Parker Palmer (1997),

> In such a [subject-centered] classroom, there are no inert facts. The great thing is so alive that teacher can turn to student or student to teacher, and either can make a claim on the other in the name of that great thing.

If my students leave my classroom with a sense that there are no inert facts, I believe I have done them an important service.

References

A Private Universe (1987). Available at https://www.learner.org/resources/series28.html. Cambridge, MA: Harvard-Smithsonian Center for Astrophysics.

Bain, K. (2004). *What the best college teachers do*. Cambridge, MA: Harvard University Press.

Baxter Magolda, M. B. (1992). *Knowing and reasoning in college: Gender-related patterns in students' intellectual development*. San Francisco, CA: Jossey-Bass.

Dweck, C. (2007). *Mindset: The new psychology of success*. New York, NY: Ballantine.

Leski, K. (2015). *The storm of creativity*. Cambridge, MA: MIT Press.

Nelson, Craig (2003). Fostering critical thinking & mature valuing across the curriculum. Nashville, TN: Faculty Workshop presented at Belmont University.

Palmer, Parker (1997). *The courage to teach: Exploring the inner landscape of a teacher's life*. San Francisco, CA: Jossey-Bass.

Perry, William, Jr. (1998). *Forms of ethical and intellectual development in the college years: A scheme*. San Francisco, CA: Jossey-Bass.

Pinter, Robbie (2017). Thresholds, portals, and crossovers: Fantasy tropes in C. S. Lewis's *Narnia* and George MacDonald's *Lilith*. Nashville, TN: Presentation at Belmont University.

Mike Pinter, Belmont University

Using Wikis to Foster and Create Student Accountability for Learning

Wikis are a website tool with multiple functions. Typically, faculty consider their use for assignments. However, due to our class' application clinical format, we approached this as a tool to support and facilitate the learner's individual scheduling needs, to tackle the semester assignments, reinforce control with the learner and ~~reinforce~~ promote a growth mindset. The practicum component of this class is individualized for each student, by the number of students registered, the different facility types and the use of multiple sites. Depending upon students' site assignment, they negotiate with the onsite fieldwork supervisor to enact a schedule to complete the course requirements for success in their fieldwork experience. Students made a calendar plan and inserted it on the course wiki within the Blackboard shell. Throughout the semester students were required to modify their visit dates based on each community site's schedule (e.g., holidays, breaks, vacations). Students individually set the dates for their visits at the setting and matched them to when they were to complete assignments. Each week these dates could be modified with changes made to their wiki, allowing the professor to monitor. The wiki offered the student the opportunity to practice and learn in a safe environment with faculty support and monitoring (Saxon, 2013; Weimer, 2017). Students managed their time and assignment due dates, reinforcing affective dimensions of critical thinking.

Developing an understanding of time management, due dates and responding to complex system demands takes practice. Through deliberate use of learning tools (e.g., wikis), occupational therapy students demonstrated accountability for managing course and assignments in real time. Thus, the students were supported through promotion of accountability measures in the course structure (Bielefeld, 2018) to motivate themselves to use this capability and skill set.

After the students' first site visit, they listed on the wiki all dates of their visits (6 total), and proposed when assignments would be turned in. This took careful review of all course assignment directions to complete the schedule and forced students to lead this process.

This activity assisted students in their ability to think critically by creating clarity and relevance through the use of a deliberate structure in maintaining course roles and responsibilities. Students demonstrated accountability for managing the course, placement demands and clinical assignments.

The wiki tool allowed students to continually reinforce professional behaviors and self-determinism, creating a sense of ownership for their learning (McCombs, 2012). Student possessed the control to guide their learning experience while increasing their professional identity and competency. The structure with the wiki tool use engaged learners as full partners in the learning process, with learners assuming primary responsibility for their own choices and scheduling within the semester framework.

Through problem-solving mechanics, students moved from intellectual conformity to intellectual autonomy. The wiki allowed students to lead and command their actions, building a professional behavior that was required on the job. Students commented:

> "The Wiki allowed me to communicate more effectively with my professor and take ownership of my schedule"
> "It allowed me to get over my perfectionism as I could calmly adjust my schedule to meet the fieldwork demands"

Being a leader forced students to learn from a different point of view demonstrating intellectual integrity by holding themselves accountable to meet site and classroom deadlines. Students stated: "I like the adaptability of the Wiki as it let me pace myself and prepare daily for what was needed."

Using the wiki allows students to practice confidence in reasoning, reinforcing intellectual humility. Coming to a conclusion and expressing their thoughts builds confidence, which is required when students work full time with clients in a clinical setting, and fosters intellectual empathy for the complexities of daily routines. Paul & Elder(2008) present a template for problem-solving that aligns with the use of a Wiki. Problem solving in our use of the wiki fostered student accountability for learning, which required evaluating, anticipating and reassessing what is needed, and restating goals and timelines. As faculty, we monitored the implications of the learners' actions, provided advice to guide revision of learner strategies to meet the complexities of application of course content in the community sites, and prepared our students for future success in a healthcare setting.

References

Bielefeld, (2018, 25 January). How to help students develop personal responsibility. Mimio Educator Blog

McCombs, (2012). Developing responsible and autonomous learners: A key to motivating students. APA.

Paul, R. & Elder, L. (2008). *The miniature guide to critical thinking: Concepts and tools*. Dillon Beach, CA: The Foundation for Critical Thinking.

Saxon, D. P. (2013). Student responsibility and self-directed learning: An interview with Christine McPhail. *Journal of Developmental Education. 36*(3), 14-17.

Weimer, M. (2017, 6 September). Getting students to take responsibility for learning. *The Teaching Professor.*

Shirley O'Brien, Eastern Kentucky University
Camille Skubik-Peplaski, Eastern Kentucky University

Creating a Critical Thinking Mindset: Using Self-Reflective Teaching Questions/Directives to Enhance Learning

It would be difficult to find a more important skill to develop in higher education than critical thinking. Colleges and universities promote the varied ways their students demonstrate critical thinking, and employers seek out employees who have the greatest ability to apply critical thinking to solve complex problems. One way to enhance student critical thinking is for instructors to increase their self-reflective skills in developing and reviewing courses. Instructors who can develop courses with an intentional focus on student critical thinking will set the foundation for enhanced student learning. In addition, instructors who evaluate their courses to find areas where students struggle can better develop new learning strategies to enhance learning. Moreover, instructors who model reflective questioning in their courses and engage students in the questioning process will be teaching valuable skills for students to use in the workforce. The following set of questions can be used to infuse critical thinking throughout a course and be used as a guide to review courses.

Questions/Directives to Help Develop a Course

- What level course are you developing (110, 200, or graduate)?
    - Lower level course may have an emphasis on content and facts; whereas, higher level courses may require synthesizing data, evaluation of concepts, or the creation of new knowledge.
- How will students be thinking differently at the end of the course?
    - Knowing how students should be thinking at the end of the course will help you develop appropriate learning activities. Think about how students will be applying, analyzing, and/or evaluating course content.

- Create a spreadsheet of the percentage of your class/ course students engaged in meaningful participation.
  - Providing time for students to practice what they learned allows the instructor an opportunity to "see" student thinking and provide immediate feedback. Learning activities should be directly related to course content and ask students to explain, defend, design, and/or revise course concepts.
- What is the central idea, concept, or principle to be learned throughout the course?
  - Designing learning performances that coincide with the central organizing principle in mind will facilitate introducing, reinforcing, and mastering content.
- How will low stakes assessments be used to monitor understanding?
  - Creating multiple opportunities for students to demonstrate and build their knowledge base can facilitate a growth mindset. Providing multiple opportunities for students to categorize, modify, and/or revise material will increase ownership in their learning.
- Think about ways to design and structure opportunities for students to reflect on their learning and provide feedback on how they learn best.
  - Increasing opportunities for students to provide feedback on their learning can increase their sense of ownership and self-efficacy.

Ideas to Help Review a Course

- Create a process to review and reflect on teaching after every class.
  - Writing learning objectives for every class and journaling on how students met or did not meet objectives will create a mindset focused on student learning. Participating in institutional learning communities focused on student learning will also increase reflective learning.
- Assess student work to determine benchmarks to reach throughout the semester.
  - By reviewing and analyzing student work instructors can develop benchmarks and have a better assessment of student learning at the beginning, middle, and end of the course. Developing this skill will allow educators to know when students are truly thinking about course content in new ways and not simply paraphrasing what was stated in class or in a textbook.
- Evaluate where in the course student learning slowed or encountered a bottle neck.
  - Predicting where students struggle can help instructors develop better assignments to master complex problems.
- Invite a colleague to observe your teaching and/or actively seek out opportunities to discuss student learning.

- Engaging in professional development can help you implement new teaching strategies, share ideas, and develop into a master educator. Conducting action research on your own teaching is an excellent means to better understand the teaching and learning process.

Creating a routine of asking self-reflective teaching and learning questions along with self-reflective directives will go a long way in increasing effective teaching strategies and student critical thinking. It is also valuable to share self-reflective teaching strategies with other educators. Creating a community where the teaching and learning process is valued will only enhance the profession and, more importantly, student learning.

Michael Kiener, Maryville University of St. Louis

Group Quizzes Encourage Critical Thinking, Team-Building, and Improved Understanding

Mastering concepts in introductory courses is often difficult because many detailed processes are covered broadly and at a fast pace. I teach an introductory biology laboratory class required for allied health programs. One of the benefits of a lab class is the direct interaction with the material. The students perform biweekly lab exercises in teams. This activity is helpful for practicing concepts. The exercises complement topics that are covered in the lecture and require hands-on investigation of models or collection of data as well as analysis and knowledge integration.

Despite the integrated direct application of concepts in this lab class, I am still often looking for other ways to encourage understanding, critical thinking, and retention. Review sessions using group quizzes and immediate feedback are useful for double-checking understanding and eliminating misconceptions. Quizzes are given to the team and contain questions that are related to learning outcomes addressed during lab exercises and lecture concepts. The quizzes include questions that require recognition of concepts, application, analysis, and critical thinking.

Each group receives feedback about their work during the review session. Teams come to a decision about an answer for each question. I evaluate their responses and let them know which problems they need to continue working on. Providing immediate feedback to students as they are learning material has been shown to improve their retention of correct concepts, especially if they first give an incorrect response (Pashler et al., 2005). In some instances, I incorporate scratch-off answer sheets (Epstein) as an additional tool. These students are allowed to continue work on a question until they discover the correct answer revealed on the answer sheet by a star.

Review sessions are lively, and the students are engaged in discussion of the material and the concepts. Following the general work session, I go over the review quiz and make sure students' questions are answered. Students share comments about these sessions and say they are helpful and make them remember connecting concepts from earlier in the unit.

Formative feedback, such as the group quizzes described here, should be defined by specific goals. In this instance, one of the goals is to improve student retention on the summative test by influencing their understanding of specific concepts. Shute (2008) reviews characteristics to consider when using formative feedback. Is it given after a student attempts a solution? Does it validate a student's answer, and indicate what should be modified? Shute (2008) also recommends that quality feedback considers the student's learning level, is less complex, and is often linked to a low-stakes assignment.

Group review sessions that incorporate corrective feedback help to eliminate internalized misconceptions. Verbal and written corrective feedback that corrects student deficiencies and eliminates student misconceptions improves learning across age-groups (Chilcoat, 1988; Lysakowski and Walberg, 1982). Dihoff (2004) has also shown that immediate correction of misconceptions using scratch-off answer sheets can prevent students from internalizing incorrect information and increases their performance.

Team review also increases interaction between group members. It encourages discussion of concepts. I have observed peer feedback and teaching while groups re-evaluate their answers. Corrective feedback also provides a record of the team's thinking process, and I have seen improved retention on summative tests. Group review quizzes that incorporate feedback help focus students' efforts on specific learning objectives. This team activity is a useful tool that can encourage critical thinking and improve student retention of scientific concepts.

References

Chilcoat, G.W. (1988). Developing student achievement with verbal feedback. *NASSP Bulletin, 72*, 8-13.

Dihoff, R., Brosvic, G., Epstein, M. & Cook, M. (2004). Provision of feedback during preparation for academic testing: Learning is enhanced by immediate but not delayed feedback. *The Psychological Record, 54*, 207-31.

Lysakowski, R. S., & Walberg, H. J. (1982). Instructional effects of cues, participation, and corrective feedback: A Quantitative Synthesis. *American Educational Research Journal, 19*, 559-572.

Pashler, H., Cepeda, N., Wixted, J. & Rohrer, D. (2005). When does feedback facilitate learning of words? *Journal of Experimental Psychology, 31*, 3-8.

Shute, V.J. (2008). Focus on formative feedback. *Review of Educational Research, 78*, 153-189.

Heather R. Wilkins, University of Cincinnati, Blue Ash College

Five-Step Process for Teaching Critical Thinking

In our advanced classes, many of our learning outcomes pertain to critical thinking – compare and contrast, analyze, evaluate – but few students enter our class prepared to meet these challenges. Over the years, we have honed a simple, five-step process that we implement in our courses, allowing students to develop the skills necessary to use evidence to make better decisions. These five steps can be built into the course design or simply used as the foundation for one or more days of discussion. We find it's best for students to be given the five steps as a handout or for the steps to be written on the board. We will begin by describing the basic process and how we've implemented it in our courses.

Our five-step process always begins with a question; that is, **step one of the process is to identify a problem.** You may have students develop their own problem or identify a problem for them. For less advanced students, we typically identify a question or problem for them. Since we teach clinically-related psychology courses, one question that has worked well is, do vaccines cause autism? For more advanced students, we may initially identify a problem, working through the five-step process with them – modeling – before having them work independently (or in small groups) on a problem they have identified.

Step two of the process involves gathering of evidence. At this point, we do not limit where students gather their evidence. Students may include websites, magazine articles, newspaper articles, scholarly journal articles, or even their neighbor.

The third and fourth steps involve evaluating the evidence. We split this into two steps to assist students in understanding the process. First, we begin with summarizing all evidence that argues on one side of the question. For example, we might begin with all evidence that indicates that vaccines *do* cause autism. For each bit of evidence, we discuss the source of the evidence, including such elements as whether the author has any expertise in this area, whether the source is peer reviewed, whether the evidence is personal opinion or based on research data, and, if the evidence is based on research data, if those results have been replicated. Initially, we walk through this process with students to model how each question should be addressed. We also provide students a written copy of these questions for them to use. By the end of this third step, we are able to summarize the information in a clearer manner. The fourth step involves completing the same process on the other side of the question, in this case, the claim that vaccines *do not* cause autism.

The fifth and final step of this process involves answering the question. With a clearly outlined summary of the evidence and the quality of the evidence on each side of the question, students discuss whether the question can be answered. In most cases, students are then able to use the evidence to argue for one side of the argument. This process is not always pretty. Some students begin the process firmly committed to one side of the question or the other. For example, some students may firmly believe that vaccines cause autism and may have chosen not to vaccinate their own children. Some of these students are the most vehement during this final step of the process. The converts – based on the evidence – are frequently livid that they were mistaken, and others – what we call the die-hards – remain convinced that they were correct despite all evidence to the contrary. Fortunately, the die-hards are less frequent.

In our classes, we frequently use this process early in the semester as a way of helping students think through developing their own research papers. Does it work? That is, does this process influence the quality of the arguments seen in their research paper? Definitely! Almost all students develop papers that present at least two sides of the issue they address and evaluate the validity of the sources they use. This is a step in the right direction.

Robin K. Morgan, Indiana University Southeast
Nate Mitchell, Spalding University

Edward de Bono's Six Thinking Hats, an Instructional Method to Teach Critical Thinking

In this article the authors will discuss one instructional method, The Six Thinking Hats of Edward de Bono, and that they have used to teach a specific kind of critical thinking to their graduate students in a course entitled Encouraging Skillful, Creative and Critical Thinking. In this course our students experience and then evaluate several critical thinking instructional methods and also discuss how these methods can be taught to their students.

Before we explain The Six Thinking Hats of Edward de Bono, let us first define critical thinking.

For the purposes of this paper, we define critical thinking as an active, purposeful, organized, cognitive process we use to carefully examine our thinking and the thinking of others in order to clarify and improve our understanding. However, in this article we will describe one specific instructional method, Edward de Bono's Six Thinking Hats, to teach a certain kind of critical thinking, the cognitive ability to understand and articulate several valid ways of solving a complex problem, such as determining the role of human behavior in climate change.

We will now present de Bono's Six Thinking Hats.

De Bono's Six Thinking Hats

With de Bono's Six Thinking Hats students learn six different ways of thinking about a problem. The six thinking hats are used to unscramble and sharpen thinking so that students are able to use one thinking mode at a time --- instead of trying to do everything all at once. By putting on different thinking hats students are stimulated to think in six different ways. See the example below

A simple way to teach the six thinking hats or perspectives is to state them as questions. As an example, let's assume the teacher wants his/her students to learn six different ways to discuss the controversial issue: should marijuana be legalized so that doctors can prescribe it for certain medical conditions?

Color of the Hat	Type of Thinking	Exemplary Question
White	Factual	What are the facts about the effects of dispensing medical marijuana to certain patients?
Red	Emotional	What do you feel about dispensing medical marijuana to certain patients?
Yellow	Positive	What do you like about dispensing medical marijuana to certain patients?
Black	Negative	What's wrong with dispensing medical marijuana to certain patients
Green	New or Innovative	What might be a fresh approach to dispensing medical marijuana to certain patients?
Blue	Theoretical or Foundational	What's the big picture about dispensing medical marijuana to certain patients?

The teacher places students into six thinking hat groups and each group discusses how to present the most cogent arguments from the perspective of their assigned thinking hat. The members of each thinking hat group are tasked with making certain that each member of each thinking hat group understands its particular point of view and can articulate that perspective during a classroom discussion facilitated by the teacher. After the classroom discussion has been completed, the teacher can assign students to write in their own words a narrative describing the six different positions on the controversial topic and then present their views on the topic.

In this article the authors described one specific instructional method, the Six Thinking Hats of Edward de Bono, to explain how this method can enable students to generate and appreciate multiple ways of solving a challenging problem. This Six Thinking Hats is one of several instructional methods including Constructive Controversy (Johnson 2015), Group Investigation (Sharan & Sharon, 1992), Co-op Co-op (S. Kagen, 2009, Send-A-Problem (S Kagen, 2009), and Spectrum of Opinion (R and E Solomon, 2012) that the authors teach in their graduate course, Enhancing Skillful, Creative and Critical Thinking. This course is designed to empower teachers to experience, evaluate, and ultimately to implement critical thinking instructional methods in their respective classrooms.

References

de Bono, E. (1985). *Six thinking hats*. Boston, MA: Little, Brown & Co.

Johnson, D W. (2015.) *Constructive controversy: Theory, research, practice.* Cambridge, England: Cambridge University Press.

Sharan, Y. & Sharan, S. (1992). *Expanding cooperative learning through group investigation.* New York, NY: Teacher's College Press.

Kagan, S. & Kagan, M. (2009). *Kagan cooperative learning.* San Clemente, CA: Kagan,

Solomon, R. & Davidson, N. (2012). *Encouraging skillful, critical and creative thinking: Participant's guide.* Tucson, AZ: Fourth R Consulting.

Richard D Solomon, University of Maryland (retired)
Neil Davidson, University of Maryland, Professor Emeritus

Increasing Critical Thinking Skills and Course Success through Co-requisite Courses

Co-requisite instruction in U.S. higher education has been largely confined to developmental English and mathematics courses. The idea behind this approach is to provide supplemental instruction in a co-requisite course to improve success in the credit-bearing course. This model can be an effective for developmental instruction, but there are opportunities to adopt a similar approach to non-developmental courses that are sequential in nature or share similar information or course concepts. A discussion of a proposed co-requisite model with introductory statistics and research methods courses follows.

Problem

Introductory statistics is a vital prerequisite for research methods courses in social sciences and natural sciences departments in colleges and universities across the U.S. Introductory statistics courses are typically taken the semester before a research methods course, providing students with the necessary statistical background knowledge to succeed in research methods. However, a common complaint by research methods faculty is that students have forgotten necessary statistical concepts and practices or that they do not know how to think critically about such concepts and apply them to research. This challenge may cause research methods faculty to have to reteach statistical concepts and practices, taking valuable time away from research methods instruction.

Students routinely report introductory statistics courses to be among their most challenging. In addition to the difficult formulas and statistical concepts, learning statistics can be problematic because it may not be clear to students what the utility of statistical knowledge is, such as how statistical concepts and practice may be applied in future college coursework or future careers. Introductory statistics faculty may not have the class time or expertise to delve into these applications, leaving students to tackle the mathematical aspects of statistics without a robust understanding of application or real world utility. A lack of preparation in practical application of statistics hinders the development of students' critical thinking about statistics and its uses. This problem can set them behind as they begin research methods coursework, which requires the application of statistical knowledge and concepts.

Solution

A solution to these challenges may be to require students to take introductory statistics in the same semester as research methods in a co-requisite model. The benefits for offering these courses as co-requisites are twofold: 1) Research methods faculty will no longer have the concern of students' knowledge of statistics fading between semesters and 2) Students can learn foundational statistical knowledge and concepts and begin to think critically about applications of statistics, such as in performing research, in the same semester.

It is important to note, however, that simply requiring introductory statistics and research methods as co-requisites may not lead to student success in either course without intentional course design and careful concept sequencing by the faculty teaching each course. For this reason, it is recommended that the following steps be taken in implementing introductory statistics and research methods as co-requisite courses:

Step 1: The faculty members teaching each course must meet beforehand to carefully map out when concepts are taught during the semester. It is vital that concepts are taught in introductory statistics prior to the concept's application in research methods. If at any point the applied statistics research methods material is taught before the associated introductory statistics foundational material, students may become confused and frustrated, which will stymie the development of critical thinking and render the co-requisite approach ineffective.

Step 2: The faculty members must meet regularly during the semester to ensure that the course pacing is on track and that students are learning and applying the information in each course as the faculty have envisioned. Consistent contact between the faculty members teaching the co-requisite courses allows each faculty member to quickly make adjustments to course pacing and provides the feedback necessary to reteach a concept.

<u>Step 3</u>: Once the semester has ended, the faculty members should meet to discuss the results of the co-requisite approach. The faculty members debrief regarding what went well and what didn't, what should be adjusted, and what should be used again. If possible, student feedback about the format and activities within the co-requisite courses should be collected and considered in future course planning.

Within the general framework for co-requisite introductory statistics and research methods courses outlined above, many additional approaches could be incorporated to increase students' critical thinking and eventual course success. For example, faculty members might choose to team-teach the courses. The research methods faculty member may teach some of the introductory statistics class sessions while the statistics instructor might teach some of the research methods class sessions. This approach allows the faculty members who are experts in a particular area to provide targeted and high-level instruction in an area the other instructor may not be as knowledgeable.

Another approach for co-requisite faculty to increase students' critical thinking within each course might be to co-design the assignments for each course in such a way that supports a more introductory or basic concept in one co-requisite class to a higher-level concept in the other co-requisite class. In discussing and eventually instituting co-requisite courses, faculty will likely discover a multitude of ways to expand instructional approaches and activities within and between each course to increase student learning, critical thinking, and eventual course success.

Jonathan W. Carrier, Laramie County Community College
Shannon Zavorka, Laramie County Community College

Modifying Project-Based Learning Concepts for Laboratory Settings

Project-based learning (PBL) is a proven active learning strategy that not only increases long-term retention of content, but also encourages critical thinking and improves student attitudes towards education (Vega, 2012). The ultimate goal of PBL is increased student learning of important knowledge and skills by confronting a messy, real-world problem and then using sustained inquiry, student choice, collaboration, and reflection to accomplish this learning goal (Buck Institute for Education, 2015). Unfortunately, PBL methods often are difficult to incorporate in hard-science subjects such as Chemistry, Physics, and Biology because the concepts frequently present problems that are closed-ended and leave little room for divergent thinking and student input. To overcome these challenges, PBL must be modified so that it both accommodates the singular-answer nature of many scientific concepts and also allows learners to use their own ideas when solving hard sciences questions. The natural setting to employ this altered hard-sciences version of PBL is in the laboratory, where students are already using active-learning strategies.

Like any teaching method, labs in and of themselves are not necessarily effective tools for promoting critical thinking in students. Thus, instructors should keep in mind a few basic questions that ensure maximization of learning in a laboratory setting. Questions that promote a well-designed lab include: 1) How can I ensure that this lab is linked to lectures? 2) What questions will deepen my students' understanding of the material? and 3) Would students benefit from a brief handout summarizing key points? (Vanderbilt University, 2018). Asking these questions when designing a lab sets the stage for optimizing student critical thinking and learning.

Although implementing these questions in the early phases of lab design provides a solid foundation for augmenting critical thinking, the structure of the lab itself is crucial. In a powerful study released by scientists from Stanford University and the University of British Columbia, Holmes, Bonn, and Wieman (2015) found that small tweaks during the lab can make significant differences in student learning. They devised an experimental study using introductory physics students. In one condition, students completed the lab in a traditional manner by following a set of instructions and comparing their result to an expected outcome. In the second condition, students followed the same instructions and utilized the same material. However, these students were then asked to explain discrepancies between their data and the given correct answers and brainstorm slight modifications that might increase the accuracy of their findings. Finally, this second group of students were asked to redo the lab with these modifications and determine whether the implemented changes improved their data. Students from the second group were an astonishing twelve times more likely to notice ways to strengthen their experiment than those in the control group. Furthermore, the experimental group was much more likely to identify possible weaknesses and limitations of experimental procedures. Most significantly, these students applied these newly developed critical thinking skills over a year later in a different class. In other words, students benefited greatly from redoing a lab after asking themselves the following question: What are some factors that could have affected the accuracy of my results (Holmes, Wieman, & Bonn, 2015)?

Students often struggle with divergent thinking in hard science classes due to the singular-correct-answer scenario. Thus, the most troublesome aspect of applying PBL strategies in hard sciences is the inclusion of student choice. However, encouraging student generation of possible solutions to solving a lab problem allows for students to make some choices and have some ownership about their work. The other characteristics of PBL, including sustained inquiry, authentic real world problems, collaboration, and reflection, can be utilized with minimal alteration. In summary, PBL strategies can be an effective method to enhance student critical thinking in traditional science classes.

References

Buck Institute for Education (2018). *Why project based learning.* Retrieved from http://www.bie.org

Holmes, N., Wieman, C., & Bonn, D. (2015, September 8). *Teaching critical thinking: Proceedings of the National Academy of Sciences.* Retrieved from http://www.pnas.org/content/112/36/11199

Vanderbilt University Center for Teaching (2018). *Teaching laboratory classes.* Retrieved from https://cft.vanderbilt.edu/guides-sub-pages/lab-classes

Vega, V. (2012). *Project-based learning research review/Edutopia.* Retrieved from http://www.edutopia.org/pbl-research-learning-outcomes

Zachary Scott, Berea College
DeDe Wohlfarth, Spalding University

Applying Critical Thinking within Administrative Contexts: Perspectives from Two Programs

Administrative Contexts in Two Programs

Administrators apply critical thinking skills and strategies daily in their leadership work. The authors both administer large writing and communication centers that facilitate related and complex teaching and learning programs for students at their academic institutions. Both founded their centers: The Naugle CommLab at the Georgia Institute of Technology (Georgia Tech) and the Noel Studio for Academic Creativity at Eastern

Kentucky University (EKU). As the authors have experienced, founding a center is an exciting opportunity. It is also an exhausting and emotional experience. The investment, professional and personally, in doing this work looms large long after center work settles into a productive pace. However, center life, and the life of center directors, is ever-changing. As our two centers have evolved, and the work within them has expanded, there are often inevitable needs to not only sustain productivity in programs, research, development, and service but also to ensure that structures are best suited to respond to institutional needs and changes. Success can lead to additional funding and the need to hire (or promote) professionals into new administrative and leadership roles. Founding (or long serving) directors must guard against letting their epistemological preferences create barriers to change and growth. In this practical contribution, two founding directors examine critical thinking strategies they have employed in administrative decision making in their centers and programs and what has "worked" in the evolution of these spaces.

Thinking critically as an administrator involves layered and diverse approaches. These approaches intersect with leadership, collaboration, and creative decision-making. The authors offer strategies in the form of critical thinking skills for use in a variety of administrative context based on lessons learned from founding and directing their centers.

7 Critical Thinking Skills for Administration

The following seven critical thinking skills can be applied and adapted for use in a variety of administrative and leadership scenarios.

Analyzing

For the founding of a center, this skill is mostly about what we perceived the needs of our centers to be, but also what we *hoped* our centers could be. This skill involves critical thinking via analysis in these areas:
- State of the field
- Needs and expectations
- Current trends

Applying Standards

In both cases, the authors brought experiences gained working in other centers, designing previous programs, and piloting techniques. We were also informed by theoretical and praxis work we studied as scholars. Our "standards" arose from these two areas.
- Identifying standards and evaluating outcomes

- Creating buy-in among co-researchers, stakeholders, and student partners

Discriminating

While both the Noel Studio and CommLab we were granted many (if not most) of the resources we needed for our centers, we still had to make choices. Some of these decisions were linked to building/facilities-based issues. In the Noel Studio, decisions were made as to scale, timeline, and outcomes, and critical thinking was applied to staffing, training, and spatial opportunities. In CommLab it was also necessary to balance institutional politics of space (the center originated as part of a large new learning commons); decisions about ownership and management were not always autonomous.

Information Seeking

For the evidence-based arguments, we used information about other centers, but also highlighted scholarship about teaching and learning. While we often made good arguments, structural decision making--like where in the building we are located--can be challenging until usage patterns and observations are available and apparent. Critical thinking should involve:
- Administrative sites for gathering information;
- Affiliation with regional and national networks; and
- Regular sharing, updating, and research with centers and colleagues of similar and different contexts.

Logical Reasoning

Using a critical thinking approach to administration can provide logical reasoning for decision making. Because of the STEM culture at Georgia Tech, special care needed to be taken to avoid any rationales that seemed anecdotal or emotional (gut feelings, for example). At EKU, decisions were made based on available information, student or faculty input, and pilot studies that allowed critical thinking via logical reasoning.

Predicting

This was the most creative component of the critical thinking process. For CommLab--because a writing center was a new concept at Georgia Tech--thinking critically about what would or could happen was often a purely creative effort. Extrapolation--either from similar internal programs or from other institutions--regarding perceived needs or outcomes was necessary. In some cases, the authors compared available data or results at their institutions, which allowed for critical thinking to emerge.

Transforming Knowledge

For our centers, we are particularly disposed to spend a great deal of time on this part of critical thinking. We are, by our very natures, a group of people who reflect and revise constantly. Being able to try new strategies or approaches, but also "pull the plug" quickly if they don't "work," is important. Thus, the authors:
- Use critical thinking to transform knowledge; and
- Apply critical thinking when engaging peers, colleagues, students, and researchers in administration

Applying Critical Thinking in Administration

In many ways, administrative leadership depends upon the ability to be especially good at the last three of these skills. Communicating rationale, predicting needs and outcomes, and reinventing as needed are the necessary jobs of directors. Others can help with the earlier strategies. Being founding directors, it is critical to separate yourself from a special kind of ownership in favor of critical thinking that is a balance of analytical, objective, data-informed, and intuitive, while maintaining a focus on strategic plans, program outcomes, and staff configurations. Critical thinking is the most effective way to facilitate objective separation and to maintain a focus on program goals and outcomes.

The authors encourage administrators to apply these critical thinking approaches in their own work. They can be adapted or repurposed in a variety of academic and institutional contexts. When applying critical thinking, administrators should consider:
- Long- and short-term outcomes;
- Inter- and intra-program benefits and drawbacks; and
- Opportunities for scholarship, data collection, and reflection that allow new pathways for critical thinking to emerge.

Critical Thinking Cases

As you consider ways in which these critical thinking approaches can be applied to your administrative contexts, consider these two cases. How might you apply the 7 critical thinking strategies?
1. Your program has the opportunity to design a new space. The space is larger than the one used for your current operations. What critical thinking strategy might you use first and why?

2. The institution where you work is undergoing a restructuring plan. How can you use critical thinking strategies offered here to analyze potential implication for your program?

Karen Head, Georgia Institute of Technology
Russell Carpenter, Eastern Kentucky University

III. Strategies: An Overview

Critical thinking strategies are less general than approaches, but not quite as specific as assignments/exercises. They translate the approaches into various courses of action. They tend to answer the question: how am I going to incorporate a given approach into my course? For instance, if the approach is to scrutinize both sides of a question, an effective strategy might be to set up a classroom debate. Another interpretation to producing diverse viewpoints might be supervised group work. A different instructor might opt for the strategy of the reflection paper. Other strategies could involve methodologies for online discussions. Some instructors develop strategies involving critical reading.

The following contributions supply you with a broad range of strategies that can be utilized intact or as a springboard for your own interpretation.

Advocacy-Inspired Critical-Thinking Practices

Advocacy as a method and mechanism for critical thinking is a powerful frame for classroom learning. By visualizing the struggles and challenges of others, students are able to problem solve and confront the real difficulties of human endeavors. Moving outside of textbook examples to meet real survivors or advocates allows for a more profound learning experience. Students are awakened in a more intense emotional process and their ability to evidence critical thinking strategies and behavior is greatly improved. Compassion for others is not only reinforced as a healthy emotional strategy, but it becomes a learning objective that can foster critical thinking and respect for the diversity of others.

Since 2016, Spalding University has been offering a course entitled Social Justice for Psychologists housed in the School of Professional Psychology. That course provides an overview of the American Psychological Association's policies on advocacy for underprivileged populations and facilitates learning-rich interactions between students, community providers and underserved populations. At the end of the course, students are required to design and participate in a group service project in the neighboring Louisville community. Community engagement pedagogies have increased in popularity over the past decade as universities embrace the potential for learning in a more active manner. Service-learning is an educational approach that combines learning objectives with community outreach. This curriculum design facilitates innovative classroom activities while simultaneously connecting students to the greater needs of their community.

In order to evaluate the impact of that course, on-going classroom data collection with self-reported measures have been administered to all of the student participants. Two separate measures of compassion are administered during the first and final classroom interactions. Those measures, the *Compassion Scale* and *Self-Compassion Scale,* were created by Dr. Kristin Neff as an evaluation of those values. The results of this on-going study continue to inform the implications and effectiveness of that service-learning course. Promoting critical-thinking, compassion and advocacy seems to be creating an impact in the classroom.

Faculty members and students in the School of Professional Psychology provide lasting service to both Spalding University and the larger community. The history of the field of Psychology is predicated on the role of the Psychologist to promote change, and that commitment to service has been formally incorporated into the American Psychological Association's Code of Ethics for Psychologists: *"Psychologists are committed to increasing scientific and professional knowledge of behavior and people's understand-*

ing of themselves and others and to the use of such knowledge to improve the condition of individuals, organizations, and society." The commitment of the field of Psychology to the improvement of the human condition is fully in line with Spalding University's articulated mission *of "meeting the needs of the times in the tradition of the Sisters of Charity of Nazareth through quality undergraduate and graduate liberal and professional studies, grounded in spiritual values, with emphasis on service and the promotion of peace and justice."*

Productive members of society have a purpose and a mission, and they create plans and goals that allow them to fulfill their potential. Recruiting and training the next generation of psychologists and health providers is an important responsibility. This is an opportunity to influence a new cohort of practitioners and impact our larger community in a positive manner. Spalding University is dedicated to helping students achieve academically, but also facilitating their sense of critical-thinking practices and compassion. These valuable qualities in life that cannot always be quantified by data or diplomas. Advocacy requires bravery and a sense of self-confidence. Aiding others in need is the larger goal of our classroom learning objectives and the heart of our educational mission.

Amy Lynn Young, Spalding University

Fostering Critical Thinking through Diversity

Study abroad programs bolster students' critical thinking skills by providing students with a more objective perception of their home and foreign countries, intercultural communication skills, and increased reflective thought, self-reliance, and self-confidence (Lee, Therriault, & Linderholm, 2012). Students gain new perspectives away from their comfort zones and in unfamiliar environments. Similar to learning a foreign language, students learn a new cultural script and synthesize seemingly unrelated information in novel ways, developing a dual perspective that is a hallmark of critical thinking (Lee et al., 2012). Overall, study abroad programs are considered a high impact practice that significantly contribute to students' personal and academic growth (Zilvinskis, 2017).

However, not all students are able to travel abroad, so researchers have examined the intellectual and personal benefits of taking multicultural classes. Well-designed interactive multicultural classes improve critical thinking, particularly in students' understanding of ideas of privilege, cultural bias, personal paradigms, and world views (Anderson, MacPhee, & Govan, 2000). Students finish such classes with a heightened awareness of racial tension, insight into their own defensiveness, and a greater level of empathy and cultural humility. Most significantly, graduated students who had taken a multicultural class were more comfortable and respectful interacting with people of different backgrounds, less judgmental of others, and demonstrated a more comprehensive awareness of poverty, ethnicity, and gender (Anderson, MacPhee, & Govan, 2000).

Just as many students cannot travel abroad, however, many also cannot take a multicultural class. For these students, we have found a practical strategy that can bring culture into our classrooms. On the first day of class, ask students two questions:

1. *What do you think sociology/psychology/general math/physics/chemistry is about?* (If you expect that students know very little about the subject matter you are teaching, you may instead include a paragraph explaining the nature of your subject matter, but be sure to leave an open-ended section where students can contradict or add to the summary definition).
2. *How do you think your cultural background, ethnicity, gender, gender identity, and sexual orientation will intersect with the material taught in this class?* If you have students who identify as white, heterosexual and cisgender, this question may be difficult for them to answer. It helps if you add a paragraph explaining: "Many white, heterosexual and cisgender (explain that cisgender means the opposite of transgender, or someone whose gender identity aligns with their biological sex), students struggle to answer this question because students who represent the "majority" often don't think about cultural issues or may not even think they have a culture. Push yourself to move past that superficial rejection of the question." Providing clear definitions for unfamiliar words like cisgender is critical to develop students' vocabulary of important multicultural terms (Blue, Mupinga, Clark, DeLuca, & Kelly, 2018).

Allow students time in class to work on the assignment, but then have them take it home to finish as their first assignment (worth a grade to ensure you have quality papers completed). When students return, intentionally pair them into dyads that cross racial, gender, and other demographic lines as much as possible. Diverse groups are critical because they enable students to experience personal stories, personalities, socio-economic backgrounds and cultural perspectives different from their own (Blue et al., 2018). After the pairs finish discussing, have each pair share a key "aha moment" with their classmates.

As a conversation starter to this discussion, you might discuss how every subject we teach interacts with culture in a myriad of wonderful ways. For example, minority students are severely underrepresented in STEM fields (Williams, 2013). This disparity reflects school district funding disparities, tracking into remedial courses, underrepresentation in advanced placement AP courses, unqualified teachers, low teacher expectations, stereotype threat, and high school retention issues (William 2013). Diverse students also experience a higher level of imposter syndrome compared to white students (Bernard, Hoggard, Neblett, & Neblett, 2018). Another noteworthy factor is that 65% of students of color report regularly experiencing microaggressions in their college classrooms, with an equal number committed by professors and students (Yosso, Smith, Ceja, & Solórzano, 2009). This rich conversation serves to intentionally welcome students marginalized by society and thoughtfully introduce others to multicultural topics.

You, as a professor, are also likely to benefit from this activity. You will strengthen your cultural humility (Tervalon & Murray-Garcia, 1998), which is the lifelong process of self-reflection and growth as we learn from other cultures. As you read your students' papers and listen to their discussions, you will change your own paradigms and cultural worldviews, thus modeling for your students how to be open to growth and willing to admit your mistakes. Modeling being a lifelong learner who can both teach others and learn from them is perhaps the most important role for you to take as you help students take the next step on their critical thinking journeys (Anderson, MacPhee, & Govan, 2000).

References

Anderson, S. K., MacPhee, D., & Govan, D. (2000). Infusion of multicultural issues in curricula: A student perspective. *Innovative Higher Education*, 25(1), 37-57.

Bernard, D. L., Hoggard, L.S., Neblett Jr., E. W., & Neblett, E. W. (2018). Racial discrimination, racial identity, and impostor phenomenon: A profile approach. *Cultural Diversity & Ethnic Minority Psychology*, 24(1), 51-61. doi:10.1037/cdp0000161.

Blue, C., Mupinga, D., Clark, A., DeLuca, V. W., & Kelly, D. (2018). Multiculturalism in the classroom. *Technology & Engineering Teacher*, 77(7), 25-31.

Lee, C. S., Therriault, D. J., & Linderholm, T. (2012). On the cognitive benefits of cultural experience: exploring the relationship between studying abroad and creative thinking. *Applies Cognitive Psychology*, 26(5), 768-778. doi:10.1002/acp.2857

Tervalon, M. & Murray-Garcia, J. (1998). Cultural humility versus cultural competence: A critical distinction in defining physician training outcomes in multicultural education. *Journal of Health Care for the Poor and Underserved*, 9(2), 117-125.

Williams, T. (2013). Being diverse in our support for STEM. *Young Adult Library Services*, 12(1), 24-28.

Yosso, T., Smith, W., Ceja, M., & Solórzano, D. (2009). Critical race theory, racial microaggressions, and campus racial climate for Latina/o undergraduates. *Harvard Educational Review*, 79(4), 659-691.

Zilvinskis, J.(2015). Using authentic assessment to reinforce student learning in high-impact practices. *Assessment Update*, *27*(6), 7-13. doi:10.1002/au.30040

DeDe Wohlfarth, Spalding University
Ameenah Ikram, Spalding University

Classroom Debates: The Good, The Bad, and The Anxiety-Provoking

The image of a teacher lecturing and students furiously taking notes no longer comes to mind when thinking about the modern classroom. Active learning approaches have to some extent replaced pure lecture-based classes, allowing for students to take control of their learning with guidance and support from the teacher. Proponents of these teaching techniques highlight their benefits, including the development and application of abstract thinking, problem-solving, and overall critical thinking skills (Bonwell & Eison, 1991; Kennedy, 2007; Yale Center for Teaching and Learning, 2018). Further, active learning approaches expand the traditional "one technique fits all" style of teaching by allowing a wider range of students to reach their learning goals.

Structured classroom debates are becoming a more popular form of active learning as an experiential classroom activity (Kennedy, 2007). The debate process requires students to consider both sides of a topic in preparation of the debate, despite whether arguing pro or con. Students must accurately define the problem/ topic, critically consume the information on all aspects of the topic, prioritize the importance of their information, and identify potential rebuttal arguments. The process undoubtedly involves multiple critical thinking skills, resulting in a more thorough understanding of material.

The benefits of debates are clearly supported in the research. However, in an attempt to foster critical thinking skills, professors may be inadvertently impairing students' learning. Students have unique characteristics and traits they bring into the classroom, which influence their individual learning experience, classroom dynamics, and other students' learning. Extroverted students typically enjoy more active learning approaches because they align with their preferences for group-based learning and social interactions. On the other hand, introverts typically prefer to learn independently and engage with class material on their own terms rather than be required to participate (Monahan, 2013).

In the classroom, introverted students are more likely to be overlooked because of their learning preferences. Introverted students also report preferring to have more time to process their thoughts before sharing them with the class, and this silence can create a space that extroverts too easily fill (Monahan, 2013). Additionally, introverts often experience anxiety in adapting to be more engaged and active in the class. For example, a classic psychological research study identified the Yerkes-Dodson law of learning. This law explains that while moderate levels of arousal/anxiety are optimal for learning, too high or low levels actually impair the learning process (Yerkes & Dodson, 1908). Active learning techniques, such as high intensity debates, may cause introverted students to exceed the optimal moderate level of anxiety, at which point learning and consolidation of information is significantly more difficult.

As an introverted student, I can personally confess that my first experience with a classroom debate was awful. Only four students out of the class of 20 were selected to participate in the debate, leaving the remaining students and professor to grade each debater's performance. To add to the anxiety, at the last moment the debaters discovered that the professor had a different set of topics in mind than those listed on the syllabus, for which we had prepared. While the preparation work helped build critical thinking skills, as my team thoroughly examined both sides of the topic, the application of this information in the debate format was overshadowed by my own performance anxiety. Consequently, what I remember most from the experience is the intense emotion of fear in the classroom rather than useful take-away knowledge.

In summary, debates can contribute to student learning, but only when they are well-crafted. The following recommendations may be helpful in designing class debates:

- Establish classroom participation expectations in the first class, or as soon as feasible, to create a supportive learning environment.
- When setting expectation for classroom debates, explicitly explain each side of the issue to avoid additional confusion and anxiety.
- Include most of the class, if not all students, on the debate teams to reduce the anxiety regarding performance.
- Allow student debate team members to choose the role in the debate that best suits them. For example, an introverted student may prefer to organize and prepare information to give to the student who will argue the points during the debate.
- Allow ample time to formulate each portion of the debate (i.e., introduction, rebuttals, and conclusion) to reduce time-related anxiety and to give students opportunity to fully apply knowledge and allow more introverted students time to speak.

- Be strategic and mindful about grading the debate activity. Grade students based on the structure and presentation of their argument instead of rewarding the "winning" team or "right" side.
- Give students opportunity to debrief and discuss the experience of the debate together prior to the end of the class session.
- Be open to student feedback about the process to better inform future debate activities.

References

Bonwell, C. C., & Eison, J. A. (1991). *Active learning: Creating excitement in the classroom.* (ASHE–ERIC Higher Education Rep. No. 1). Washington, DC: The George Washington University, School of Education and Human Development.

Kennedy, R. (2007). In-class debates: Fertile ground for active learning and the cultivation of critical thinking and oral communication skills. *Journal of Teaching and Learning in Higher Education, 19*(2), 183-190.

Monahan, N. (2013). *Keeping introverts in mind in your active learning classroom.* Retrieved from http://www.facultyfocus.com/author/nicki-monahan/

Yale Center for Teaching and Learning (2018). *Strategies for teaching: Active learning.* Retrieved from https://ctl.yale.edu/ActiveLearning

Yerkes R.M., Dodson J.D. (1908). The relation of strength of stimulus to rapidity of habit-formation. *Journal of Comparative Neurology and Psychology, 18*, 459–482. doi:10.1002/cne.920180503.

Kelsey Stout, Spalding University
DeDe Wohlfarth, Spalding University

Using a Relic of Past Pedagogical Practices to Enhance Critical Thinking in 21st Century Classrooms

I must confess that I have a difficult time with letting go of physical items. Therefore, for several weeks I sat at my desk and stared at a relic of the past century that was left in my office by the previous tenant. The overhead projector was once touted in the 20th century as the latest in technological advances to be implemented within pedagogical practices. Now, in the 21st century, many overhead projectors sit in surplus warehouses across the country.

I made a decision that if I was to keep this relic, then I must use this relic. I asked myself, "Why not use an overhead within my classes? After all, chalkboards are still in use across the country." On my quest, I have discovered that an overhead projector can be quite useful in enhancing critical thinking. I have discovered that there are advantages to overhead projectors when compared to document cameras.

However, before using the overhead projector within a class, you must first seek out transparency paper, which may be located in the deep, dark recesses of a cabinet. Second, you need to find markers that write on transparency paper.

My favorite use of the overhead projector is to project questions or points that I want students to think about when watching a media clip within class. I found that it is quite useful to have these questions or points projected at the same time as the media clip. This action is difficult to do with a document camera, as the screen for the document camera and the media are often one and the same. However, with the overhead projector you can project the image on the wall next to the screen, thus students can continually refer to the questions or points. I purposely leave space between the questions or points, allowing me to capture thoughts of our discussion after the showing. Yes, this process can be done with the document camera or with a word document on your computer, but then when you move on with your lecture or the next media clip, the discussion is gone. With the overhead projector, you can leave the discussion thoughts up. Students can continue to reflect on the discussion and make connections to course content. Leaving the comments up also allows you to refer to the points. You can also allow students to add to them throughout the class session and even throughout the semester.

Using an overhead transparency projector allows you to encourage critical thinking throughout the class session and to assess students' thinking. Below are a few ways to implement universal intellectutual standards (Paul & Elder 2006) within your face-to-face class meetings:

Clarity

When having small group discussions, provide each group with transparency paper and marker to capture small group discussion points. This action will allow y o u to project the discussion points to share with the large group when the   small group is reporting out.

Accuracy

At the beginning of class, write the phrase "What do we need to fact check today?" on the transparency, then project it on the wall. Ask students to think about what "facts" are being provided during the lecture and if there are specific facts that they would like to verfy. Leave time for students to conduct brief research (via an electronic device), to share findings and source. This activity can also serve as a gateway to discuss credible sources.

Precision

Provide individual students with a slip of transparency paper to write a question they had during class, then take time at the end of class to display and discuss a few. Yes, students can just ask a question, but they may be hesitant. Knowing they can submit a question anonymously may encourage them to ask it.

Relevance

As a class opening or ending actiivty, write an unfinished quote or phase on the transparency, project it on the wall, ask students to think about it during class, and finish the quote or phrase. Leave time to discuss and debrief.

Depth

Provide students with a slip of transparency paper and ask them to write a six word story about a particular course concept or topic. Display the stories and discuss with the whole class.

Breadth

Provide students with a slip of transparency paper and ask them to write one word that sums up the lecture, thoughts, or concepts for class that day. Take time at end of class to display and discuss a few.

Logic

Provide students with a piece of transparency paper to capture an "ah ha" moment they had during class, then take time at the end of class to display and discuss a few.

Significance

Ask students to draw a meme to explain a central course concept. Share a few with the whole class to see if others can guess the central idea.

Fairness

Provide the students with a piece of transparency paper and ask them to think about how they have a vested interest in an issue. Then ask them to draw a flow chart or concept map connecting themselves to the issue. Share a few with the whole class to discuss the connection.

I have enjoyed the intellectual challenge of thinking of new ways to use a relic of past pedogological practices to enhance critical thinking in a 21st Century classroom. The students have responded well and seem to enjoy the various ways I have infused critical thinking into the class. As with anything that is not used very often as it once was, it does become difficult to locate items to maintain its usefulness. Therefore, I must leave you and seek out a few overhead transparency light bulbs.

Reference

Paul, R. and Elder, L. (2006). *The miniature guide to critical thinking concepts and tools.* The Foundation for Critical Thinking. Retrieved from https://www.criticalthinking.org/files/Concepts_Tools.pdf

Mary A. Sciaraffa, Eastern Kentucky University

Applying Visualization Techniques to Literacy Instruction

High-Impact Practice Addressed: Collaborative Assignments and Projects

Developing preservice early childhood educators (PECE) who understand the importance of reader response activities (Rosenblatt, 1978) in the development of comprehension skills can be a daunting task, especially since many educators find it difficult to remember how they learned to read and understand the written word. The role of the teacher educator, then, is to simulate those experiences in order to help PECE understand the role of pedagogical tools such as visualization and subsequent graphic representations in the form of "storyboards" (Wilhelm, 1997) or illustrative drawings (Eisenkraft, 1999; Smagorinsky, 1997).

Visualization is one of the seven "big ideas" in reading comprehension (Pearson et al, 1992). Most researchers and practitioners agree that there are seven core strategies for the development of reading comprehension in young readers. These include activating background/prior knowledge, questioning the text, drawing inferences, evaluating text structure, creating mental images, metacognition and repair strategies, and synthesizing information. Creating mental images, also called visualization, indicates the skill by which readers constantly create mind pictures as they read, developing images in their head of the actions, characters, or themes.

Teachers, especially those who work with beginning or emerging readers, use picture books with students, not only because the text is simple and they are easy to read, but because the opulent and detailed art in this type of book can assist students in seeing how words and images connect in the meaning-making process of reading. While educators may continue to utilize pictures books throughout the educational process and across grade levels and content areas, around the third or fourth grades, students begin to encounter text that is denser, more sophisticated, and less graphic in nature, such as content area textbooks and chapter books. As a result, students must learn to create their own mental images in the absence of book illustrations.

PECE are taught the seven core strategies in the literacy coursework of their teacher education programs. As part of elucidating how the visualization strategy works, PECE are required to read Edgar Allan Poe's *The Masque of the Red Death* (Poe, 1910). This 2,453-word short story, although written at a 7.0 level on the Flesch-Kincaid readability scale, is a dense text full of graphic imagery of the main character, Prince Prospero, his imperial suite of seven uniquely-decorated rooms, and the masqueraders invited to the ball in the wake of a pestilence called "the red death" raging outside the castle walls. PECE are required to read the text silently and then subsequently develop a storyboard of at least 10 frames.

A storyboard is a graphic organizer that is similar to a cartoon strip. It can be used as a way to plan a narrative or to organize a future video or production, but, in this case, it is used to retell a narrative story graphically. The linear orientation tells a story, explains a process, or illustrates the passage of time. By PECE breaking the larger story into bite-sized chunks, readers are able to focus on the elements of each cell (or aspect of the story) separately. The parameters of the Poe storyboard that the PECE must create are bifurcated: 1) each frame must include an exact quote from the text; 2) each frame must include a rich, full-colored illustration of that quote that represents the reader's image of what the quote "says." At the completion of the project, PECE must share their storyboards with the class, explain why they chose the quotes they used, and then write a three-paragraph reflection about the significance of the literacy strategy for use with their future students.

As a follow-up to the in-class visualization activity, PECE are required to secure a text that they could use for a visualization lesson with their target grade level (PreK-3).

The text may not be a picture book, which is the most common reading material used with young children. Instead, it should be a text devoid of graphic representations so that it will require the young readers (or listeners) to develop their own mental images. Examples might include a short story without illustrations, or an alternative text, such as song lyrics or poem that are both age- and developmentally- appropriate. PECE will write a lesson plan for a visualization activity that utilizes that text as a focal point of the instruction.

The assignment simultaneously requires PECE to think critically about the visualization process as a tool for reading comprehension and equips them with an effective, real-world exercise that can be used in the classroom.

References

Eisenkraft, S. I. (1999). A gallery of visual responses: Artwork in the literature classroom. *The English Journal, 88*(4), 95-102.

Pearson, P. D., Roehler, L.R., Dole, J.A., & Duffy G. G. (1992). Developing expertise in reading Comprehension. In S. Jay Samuels & Alan Farstrup (eds.) *What research has to say about reading instruction* (2nd ed.). Newark, DE: International Reading Association.

Poe, E. A. (1910). *The works of Edgar Allen Poe* (Lit2Go Edition). Retrieved from http://etc.usf.edu/lit2go/147/the-works-of-edgar-allan-poe/5383/the-masque-of-the-red-death/

Rosenblatt, L.M. (1978). *The reader, the text, the poem: The transactional theory of the literary work.* Carbondale, IL: Southern Illinois University Press.

Smagorinsky, P. (1997). Artistic composing as representational process. *Journal of Applied Developmental Psychology, 18*(1), 87-105.

Wilhelm, J. (1997). *You GOTTA BE the book.* New York, NY: Teachers College Press

Angela M. Miller-Hargis, University of Cincinnati Blue Ash
Anamarie L. Waite, University of Cincinnati

Group Work as a Tool to Enhance Critical Thinking

Teachers play an invaluable role in improving students' thinking processes by providing explicit knowledge of how to think critically (Gillies & Khan, 2009). Group work is often used as a tool to reach this goal through an active exchange of ideas leading to new perspectives from a diverse group of peers (Gokhale, 1995). Research supports a multitude of positive impacts of group work on student learning. For example, group work encourages active thinking (Bourner, Hughes, & Bourner, 2001), incites deeper understanding of the content through application and practice (Gomez-Lanier, 2018), and improves problem solving abilities (Gokhale, 1995), all of which are considered to be essential elements of critical thinking. The real-world implications of collaborative learning are highlighted by the improvement of social and interpersonal skills, particularly the enhancement of communication and conflict management abilities (Galton, Hargreaves, & Pell, 2009; Payne, Monk- Turner, Smith, & Sumter, 2006). Research also suggests that group work results in longer retention of relevant information (Gokhale, 1995) by providing students with engaging opportunities to connect them with course content (Payne et al., 2006; Gomez-Lanier, 2018). Overall, research suggests that the implementation of group work can promote critical thinking.

Despite many benefits, students often complain about group work. One common grievance is that class time is wasted teaching the material to other students in the group who are less prepared (Gokhale, 1995). Students also mention problems negotiating conflicts within the group (Bourner et al., 2001), and the lack of direction or oversight by teachers during group projects (Gatfield, 1999). The main problem that students seem to have with collaborative learning, however, centers around the grading process associated with group work. Students report that they often feel the grades are not distributed fairly based on the amount of work done by each group participant (Gatfield, 1999). Another common complaint is social loafing, described as the reduction of effort by individuals working collectively rather than independently (Kench, Field, Agudera, & Gill, 2009). For example, a student may only attend one group meeting, but may receive the same grade on the project as a member who attended all of the meetings. A similar problem encountered by many students during collaborative projects is "free-riding." "Free-riding" occurs when a particular member of the group does not participate in the group activities, yet still gets credit for the finished product of the group (Kench et al., 1999). The typical free-riding scenario occurs when a group member continues to push off his or her assigned responsibilities in the group until other members have to step in to complete the project in order to ensure their own positive grade on the assignment. One popular method that has been suggested in order to remedy these complaints is peer assessment.

Peer assessment is one way we can maximize the benefits of group work and reduce the barriers. This grading style involves allowing the students to evaluate each group member and give each person a score based on individual contributions to the overall project (Kench et al., 2009). For example, students can fill out an online form responding to a series of statements, such as, "My peer attended all group meetings." using a scale that ranges from strongly agree to strong disagree (Kench et al., 2009).

Alternatively, students could grade their peers using a five-point Likert scale regarding specific tasks within the group assignment. Common scale responses include: (1) didn't contribute; (2) attempted contribution; (3) average; (4) contributed more than average; (5) contributed the most. Peer evaluations are then factored into each individual's total grade for the group project. Overall, peer assessment is a research-supported method of providing students with a more positive experience (Gatfield, 1999).

Increased teacher involvement has also been shown to improve student satisfaction with group assignments (Gatfield, 1999). Teacher involvement includes providing more oversight and ensuring students have clear goals and are communicating with each other and holding regular meetings (Payne et al., 2006). Teachers should also **explicitly share the benefits of collaborative learning**, as outlined in this essay, including enhancing students' communication skills, promoting critical thinking, and allowing students to practice working in teams. Peer assessment, increased teacher involvement, and sharing clearly the intended benefits of group work can help maximize learning outcomes and decrease student complaints.

References

Bourner, J., Hughes, M., & Bourner, T. (2001). First-year undergraduate experiences of group project work. *Assessment & Evaluation in Higher Education, 26*(1), 19-39.

Galton, M., Hargreaves, L., & Pell, T. (2009). Group work and whole-class teaching with 11- to 14-year-olds compared. *Cambridge Journal of Education, 39*(1), 119-140. doi:10.1080/03057640802701994

Gatfield, T. (1999). Examining student satisfaction with group projects and peer assessment. *Assessment & Evaluation in Higher Education, 24*(4), 365-377.

Gillies, R., & Khan, A. (2009). Promoting reasoned argumentation, problem-solving and learning during small-group work. *Cambridge Journal of Education, 39*(1), 7-27. doi:10.1080/03057640802701945

Gokhale, A. A. (1995). Collaborative learning enhances critical thinking. *Journal of Technology Education, 7*(1), 22. doi:10.21061/jte.v7i1.a.2

Gomez-Lanier, L. (2018). Building collaboration in the flipped classroom: A case study. *International Journal for the Scholarship of Teaching and Learning, 12*(2). doi:10.20429/ijsotl.2018.120207

Kench, P. L., Field, N., Agudera, M., & Gill, M. (2008; 2009;). Peer assessment of individual contributions to a group project: Student perceptions. *Radiography, 15*(2), 158-165. doi:10.1016/j.radi.2008.04.004

Payne, B., Monk-Turner, E., Smith, D., & Sumter, M. (2006). Improving group work: Voices of students. *Education, 126*(3), 441-448.

Sarah Chatt, Spalding University
Keanu Hackley, Spalding University
DeDe Wohlfarth, Spalding University

Do Reflection Papers Facilitate Critical Thinking?

As a doctoral student just beginning to teach, I want to ensure I design classes solidly built on best practice teaching literature. My biggest debate was the pros and cons of requiring reaction papers versus administrating weekly quizzes. I know from being a student that although quizzes motivate me to read, they are often anxiety provoking and thus interfered with my learning and remembering information. I strongly preferred reaction papers that required me to briefly summarize the assigned reading and integrate it with other ideas or apply it to my life as I believed this led to my longer term retention of the material and deeper critical thinking. However, was my favoring reaction papers over quizzes just a personal preference or rooted in the literature?

A 2008 study by Ferguson examined the use of student feedback on reflection papers in order to assess students' developing critical thinking skills. Participants were students from five separate World Religion classes over a five-year period. Each student in every class wrote ten reflection papers over the reading and then applied the reading to their own lives while also analyzing, interpreting, and evaluating the material. After the class was completed, students filled out a survey to identify the pros and cons of the reflection paper process. Ferguson's qualitative study found that the students believed the reflection papers encouraged critical thinking, gave them an outlet to express their personal opinions, helped them study for tests, enabled them to understand class topics more in depth, and overall allowed them to stay prepared for class on a week-by-week basis (Ferguson, 2008). However, a limitation of the Ferguson study is that it relied on self-report data and offered no "head to head" competition of reaction papers versus quizzes.

A follow up 2011 study by Bleicher examined how students felt about different components of a college course. In this study, students reported they "hated" completing all the writing assignments. However, despite this complaint, most students requested more writing and reflection paper assignments instead of tests and quizzes. While the students reported disliking the required copious time and commitment the writing assignments took, they reported the process improved their understanding of the material and overall ability to reason. They also reported enjoying hearing other students' opinions and their understanding of the reading (Bleicher, 2011).

These two studies suggest that students believe completing reflection papers helps develop their critical thinking skills. However, two studies that focus on students' perceptions of learning, and not true measures of learning itself, are hardly sufficient support to build a pedagogical philosophy and design a class. Stronger quantitative studies need to be completed to overcome the challenges of self-report research. As for me, I will use reflection papers as assignments in my classes instead of quizzes. Given no solid pedagogical reason to choose one type of assignment over the other, personal preference will carry the day.

References

Bleicher, E. (2011). The last class: Critical thinking, reflection, course effectiveness, and student engagement. *Honors in Practice, 130,* 39-52.

Ferguson, M. (2008). Use of student feedback on reflection papers to assess critical thinking. *Mountainrise, A Journal of Teaching and Learningm, 1,* 1-13.

Annie Baumer, Spalding University

Making it Relevant: Building Online Discussions

We're not sure what is worse in an online course – death by PowerPoint, the curse of the talking heads, or the mind-numbing discussion forums. Of course, none of these is necessary! Consider the online discussion forum. Some experts have argued that discussion forums (also known as discussion boards or threaded discussions) might be one of the most commonly used tools in online learning. Many instructors post a prompt to which students must respond within a specified time period. Subsequently, students must respond to one or two of their peers also within a specified time period. Ideally, the role of the instructor in a discussion forum is to encourage students to reflect critically on the topic of the discussion.

What actually happens? The problem typically begins with the discussion forum prompt created by the instructor. A discussion forum that begins with a prompt that has a single "correct" answer doesn't generate much discussion. The best discussion forum prompts are thought provoking. Consider the following two discussion forum prompts:
- List the stages of sleep and when sleepwalking is most likely to occur.
- If a sleepwalker commits a crime, should they be held legally liable?

Which of these two prompts might be of more interest to you? We think most of us would choose the second prompt even though it might be harder to answer. That is, it's relatively easy to look up the stages of sleep in your textbook and locate in which stage sleepwalking is most likely to occur. This prompt is essentially asking for factual information that can be easily located. Now, consider the second prompt. Answering this prompt is not as easy. It requires students to consider what they have learned about sleepwalking and consider how this relates to criminal liability. Students may need to seek additional resources to address this prompt; their textbook may not include all of the elements needed. Students may also reach different conclusions based on their evaluation of the evidence they located.

The second prompt, we might argue, would lead to more engaging discussions and require students to participate in higher-level critical thinking. Perhaps. We would want to be sure the instructor reviews student postings, adding comments and suggestions to ensure students are moving in an appropriate direction. We would also want to be sure grading criteria clearly provide students detailed expectations about how to respond to their peers so that peer-to-peer responses further discussion. To accomplish these tasks, the creation of a grading rubric that clearly outlines expectations is necessary. Such a rubric must place value on both the quality of peer-to-peer responses and the higher-level critical thinking skills you desire students to demonstrate.

A final step may be necessary though. Even a prompt such as the second one of our examples may not be sufficient. Students may not have any experience of a person who has committed a crime while sleepwalking and may be disbelieving that this act is realistic. Therefore, although the prompt may be relevant to the course content, the best discussion prompts are also connected to current events. Consider this prompt: Roseanne Barr recently claimed that her inappropriate tweets were due to Ambien. How does Ambien impact sleep? Is it possible that we can engage in behaviors while sleeping or under the influence of a drug such as Ambien without our knowledge? Should we be held accountable for our behavior while sleeping or taking a sleep medication such as Ambien?

Would you be interested in responding to this prompt? Would you be interested in reading what your fellow students had written? Our own results suggest that students provide lengthier and more reflective responses to prompts such as this. This last prompt is relevant to the course, brings in current events, and requires students to integrate material from several possible sources. However, students should be able to address the prompt without spending weeks researching the topic. Creating prompts such as this one may mean instructors think carefully about current events and how they relate to their course. Currently, we keep a collection of discussion prompts that have worked well in our online courses. When we hear about a relevant current event, we update the prompt. Having a collection of prompts allows us to vary the ones we use each semester, which is helpful for those students who may be re-taking the course. Alternatively, with advanced students, one could assign them a given week/chapter/topic and have them be in charge of developing an online discussion considering all of the elements of the last prompt. If considering this option, we recommend making sure you review their prompts a week prior to their assigned posting to ensure quality and provide feedback and/or time for revision. We have found that many advanced students are excited to find current events that spark debate and critical thinking, which may be more relevant to their daily lives.

Robin K. Morgan, Indiana University Southeast
Nate Mitchell, Spalding University

What Flavor Are Your Questions?

As teachers we're very accustomed to asking our students questions. Questions, however, come in different flavors. Let's think about ice cream for a moment. For us, the decision on an ice cream flavor is dependent on the context and desired outcome. For example, when we want apple pie a la mode, we frequently select vanilla ice cream. The vanilla ice cream complements the apple pie without distracting from the overall purpose of the dessert. So, while vanilla is perfectly fine with apple pie, when we crave ice cream by itself, we usually seek more complex flavors such as pralines and cream or black cherry chocolate chip. Similarly, the 'flavor' of questions we ask as teachers should depend on what we are trying to achieve.

For the most part, instructors tend to ask what we would call clarifying questions. That is, questions such as:

- What resources did you use for this project?
- How did X explain that?
- What happened in that situation?
- What did it mean when the author said X?

In many cases, when we ask our students questions, we ask students for facts. Our questions simply provide students cues about the specific facts we want them to regurgitate. In many cases, clarifying questions have a single "correct" response.

There is nothing inherently wrong with asking clarifying questions. As instructors, we need our students to be able to define and identify the content of the course. Clarifying questions can assist students in identifying what is important in the readings or lectures, assisting them in organizing their learning.

Is that all we want, though? Clarifying questions on their own do as not prepare students for higher-level critical thinking. A different type of question, the probing question, may be a better choice to help students think more deeply about the content. What is a probing question? A probing question asks students to take the information they have learned and think about it differently. Consider questions such as:
- Why do you think X happened?
- What do you think would happen if …?
- How did you determine that X was correct?
- What is the connection between X and Y?
- What if the opposite was true? Then what?

In each of these examples, the probing question is constructed in such a way that multiple answers are possible. In essence, the best probing questions are open-ended and ask students to solve a problem based on what they have learned. These types of questions encourage reflection, perspective taking, and critical thinking.

Since we teach psychology, we'll provide a brief example that might occur in one of our own courses. In our abnormal psychology courses, our goal is for students to be able to diagnose disorders based on short vignettes, review relevant etiological theories, and provide details about the most effective treatments for the disorder. As students debate which treatment might be most effective, we might ask a clarifying question such as, *"What are the components of systematic desensitization?"* This is a great question, as we want students to understand this treatment strategy. However, students are more challenged by a probing question such as, *"What would happen if relaxation wasn't added?"* This latter question forces students to consider the various components of systematic desensitization and whether all of these components are necessary for treatment success. Students may need to conduct additional research to determine what happens when various components of systematic desensitization are modified, leading them to a greater understanding of the underlying mechanisms of this strategy.

We have rarely encountered a "bad" flavor of ice cream. Yet, thoughtful consideration of flavors has allowed us to move pass the simplicity of vanilla towards delightful complexity. Similarly, thoughtful consideration of our questions has allowed our students to move pass the simplicity of facts towards the very often delightful complexity of critical thinking!

Robin K. Morgan, Indiana University Southeast
Nate Mitchell, Spalding University

Engaging Critical Thinking in Online Discussions

Online discussion forums are ubiquitous; almost every online course utilizes some type of discussion forum. Although the use of online discussions is frequently described as a best practice in teaching online, students and faculty alike can be heard detailing the pitfalls of this pedagogical tool. For some, these pitfalls have led to a high level of annoyance or even hatred of the online discussion forum. Why the strong negative reaction? There appear to be three central features of these discussions that lead to difficulty. First, many discussion topics are not designed in such a way to create discussion, but, instead, are simply short answer or essay questions with a single correct answer. Second, expectations for student responses in online discussions are frequently unclear. This lack of clarity is only magnified by instructors providing full credit for the number of student responses rather than the quality of student responses. Finally, many instructors fail to monitor or engage in online discussion, leaving students to flounder in addressing the issue.

Resolving these issues requires a multi-step process, heavily reliant on faculty expertise and time. Fortunately, much of the work can be completed prior to the start of the class, allowing greater time to be spent engaging in discussion with students.
In our online classes, we have incorporated a 5-step process, originally developed for our face-to-face courses, as the foundation of online discussions. The five steps of this process are:

1. **Identification of a problem**: In many respects, this may be one of the most important steps in this process, especially for online discussions. A good online discussion question must allow for multiple arguments. For example, in our Sleep and Dreams course, one of our discussions focuses on sleepwalking. A possible question might be, *"Are sleepwalkers dreaming? What evidence might assist you in answering this question?"* On the surface, this looks like a good discussion question. Upon closer reflection, though, it quickly becomes apparent that there is only one correct answer to this question. If students understand the sleep cycle and when sleepwalking occurs during the sleep cycle, there is nothing much to discuss. Consider a second question, *"Should sleepwalkers be held accountable for crimes they commit while sleepwalking?"* Unlike the first question, this question has multiple possible answers based on available evidence. This second question has led to engaging and thought-provoking discussions in our Sleep & Dreams courses over the past five years.

2. **Gathering of evidence:** During this part of the process, we allow students to gather evidence from any source they would like including their friends, websites, Wikipedia, books, or scholarly articles. We will frequently provide a website or scholarly article for students to read relating to the topic, thereby ensuring that they all have at least basic research evidence.
3. **Evaluate the evidence on one side of the argument**: Students are asked to summarize the evidence they have found that would argue for one side of the argument. In the case of the sleepwalking discussion, students are explicitly asked to summarize and evaluate the evidence that would support holding sleepwalkers accountable for crimes committed while sleepwalking. In the directions for the discussion, we explicitly ask students to consider the source of the evidence, including such elements as whether the author has any expertise in this area, whether the source is peer reviewed, whether the evidence is personal opinion or based on research data, and, if the evidence is based on research data, if those results have been replicated.
4. **Evaluate the evidence on the other side of the argument:** Once students summarize the evidence for one side of the argument, they are then explicitly asked to summarize and evaluate the evidence for the other side of the argument. In the case of the sleepwalking discussion, students are explicitly asked to summarize and evaluate the evidence that would support not holding sleepwalkers accountable for crimes committed while sleepwalking.
5. **Using the evidence acquired, answer the question:** Finally, students are explicitly asked in the directions for the discussion to directly answer the question based on their evaluation of the evidence they have acquired.

Creating the discussion and providing students explicit instructions about the process is critical but not sufficient. Two additional components are required. First, we create detailed rubrics outlining how grades will be assigned. One-third of the grade is based on students effectively completing steps 2-5 of this process. The other two-thirds of their grade in the discussion is based on their responses to their peers. We specifically detail what is expected in these responses; no credit is given for responses consisting of just, "We agree." Instead, students are expected to use evidence to question their peers' conclusions, suggest alternative explanations, or present new evidence.

Even this process would not be sufficient without the final step. For an online discussion to truly engage students and enhance critical thinking, we argue that the instructor must be present in the discussion. As students begin posting in the discussion, we ask questions to clarify misunderstandings or to challenge students to consider alternative viewpoints. This action engages the students in the process and allows us to shape their responses, pointing out where their comments do not match the evidence presented or identifying gaps in their evaluation of the evidence. It's critical, though, not to stifle discussion, so we're careful not to respond to every post or to indicate if we believe what is being said is "correct" or "incorrect." What is most exciting to us as instructors is that students begin using evidence to justify their conclusions rather than simply presenting personal opinions.

Robin K. Morgan, Indiana University Southeast
Nate Mitchell, Spalding University

Cracking Open the Books: Reading to Foster Critical Thinking

Background

Critical thinking and reading have been inextricably linked since the introduction of the term "close reading" as a literary practice in the 1920's (Elder & Paul, 2004). Of course, the hope of critical thinking via reader engagement relies upon motivating undergraduates to "crack open their books." Unfortunately, recent reports indicate that the percentage of students who self-identify as readers appears to be waning (Hoeflt, 2012). As a result, instructors are challenged to develop activities that promote interacting with text, designing instruction that fortifies meta-skills alongside reading comprehension. Furthermore, to recognize and honor the importance of reading requires determining methods for evaluating and responding to students' engagement with texts (Crismore, 1987; Lee, 2017).

Contextual Reading Assignments

In preparation for their careers in an educational setting, undergraduate teacher candidates are required to read a variety of texts—from documents legislating content and evaluation standards to professional journals to research theses on best practices. As part of their junior methods course, the instructor created an online folder for each student, containing the entirety of their readings in pdf format. The preservice teachers used Acrobat Reader to annotate the pdfs, while the instructor built a computer macro for sending an email alert whenever changes/annotations were made to any documents in the shared folder. As part of the feedback loop and to foster engagement, the instructor was able to follow-up on students' responses to the readings in a variety of way, including providing comments/questions for individuals and collecting information for small- and large-group discussions.

The following table outlines how readings were harnessed to foster critical thinking, attending to the context of purpose and types of text:

Assignment	Timing	Type of Text	Follow-Up
Three Burning Questions	Prior to Reading	Theory and Research Articles	Small Group Discussions
Purpose			
To analyze research on teaching and learning through close-reading of scientific articles.			
Instructions			
After reading an abstract of the research (but prior to reading the article itself), write three questions that you hope to have answered by the end of the document (one question per index card). While reading, if you find the answer to your question, note the statement/location on the back of card. During small group discussions, you will be sharing and discussing your discoveries and/or outstanding questions.			
In-the-Moment Marking	Throughout Reading	Professional Teaching Practice Articles	Individual Responses from Instructor
To develop metacognition on teaching practices			
As you read the article, use the annotation tools to highlight passages, using the following code: blue highlights for ideas you "buy into" (I understand or I agree), red highlights for "realizations" (I never thought of that), and green highlights for "going deeper" (I am not convinced or I am not sure that I follow the thinking). In addition (and, in particular, for green highlights), use the annotation tools to type comments or questions.			
Sorting Reactions	Post Reading	Political Documents or Fictional Accounts	Large Group / Entire Class Conversations
To situate personal dispositions in relation to the ideas and beliefs of others			
Immediately after reading of the text, brainstorm your reactions for three minutes (single words or short phrases), writing your ideas on a blank sheet of paper. Allow yourself a full three minutes to squeeze out your thoughts. Circle three of your jottings that you believe will be in common (a similar view) with most people in the class. Put a box around one entry that you think to be uniquely "owned by you." Take a photo of your paper and send to me, as an attachment.			

Reflections and Implications

On end-of-semester course evaluations, students addressed the impact of the engagement activities associated with their readings. In essence, the juniors found the mode of interacting (annotating and e-commenting) to be productive and the processes (questioning, marking, and sorting) to be valuable.

> "The group discussions, with the index cards, were extremely helpful. Some of the questions that I had weren't answered, but others in the group helped me find other resources to examine. The two-heads-better-than-one theory holds!"

> "The color-coded highlighting made the strongest impact, in my opinion. I liked being able to have a pseudo-conversation with the professor. Also, I felt like it kept me the most engaged - compared to the other two reading activities.'"

> "The brainstorming and circling technique was excellent for one assignment; by the time we used it on a third reading (the abstract play on the math lesson), it became a little stale. I felt as if I was trying to be radical during my brainstorming ... and, maybe trying a bit too hard ... a little unnaturally ... to be radical. Is it really brainstorming if you are purposefully forcing yourself toward a goal (being unique or shocking or just plain different ... at the expense of losing your true identity)?"

> "So much better than simply reading and coming to class without a clue as to how the readings will be used or - in some cases - not addressed at all! In many cases I just won't do the reading if I'm unsure whether we're held accountable in some way. These techniques were good - neither carrots, nor sticks really - just some good old-fashioned trying to connect yourself to the reading."

These comments suggest that students appreciate specific approaches to engaging with texts, conveying a need for multiple strategies and a wariness of overuse. By matching the purpose, timing, and type of reading, the juniors were able to develop skills that will be put to good use in the teaching profession. In fact, being able to dissect and analyze text may be particularly useful to a new generation of teachers in an age of effortless transmission of ideas. And although this exercise was conducted in a teacher education program, it is worth noting that the ideas and procedures can work for any course looking to promote critical thinking via reading.

References

Crismore, A. (1987). *Initiating students into critical thinking, reading, and writing about texts.* ED288202.

Elder, L., & Paul, R. (2004). Critical thinking and the art of close reading, Part IV. *Journal of Developmental Education, 28*(2), 36–37.

Hoeft, M. E. (2012). Why university students don't read: What professors can do to increase compliance. *International Journal for the Scholarship of Teaching and Learning, 6*(2), article 12.

Lee, Y.-H. (2018). Scripting to enhance university students' critical thinking in flipped learning: Implications of the delayed effect on science reading literacy. *Interactive Learning Environments, 26*(5), 569–582.

Jeffrey P. Smith, Otterbein University

Think About It! – Facilitating Student Thinking with Reflective Responses

"The one who does the work does the learning." – Terry Doyle

Encouraging critical thinking in students requires giving students opportunities to do the work instead of doing it for them. The course instructor serves as an expert curator of knowledge rather than a disseminator of it. The idea is to help provide the content and context and give students the tools to apply and evaluate the content, while considering its implications within a meaningful context. In this vein we help novice students develop skills to become experts. This process may not only involve gaining expertise in a particular subject matter, but also developing into expert thinkers and learners. Instructors can require reflective responses to a range of materials including, but not limited to, readings, videos, lectures, field experiences, current news stories and podcasts. Responses may occur in a variety of ways, including in class discussion, on demand writing tasks, online discussion board postings, journal entries, or papers. Downing (2017) highlights constructing logical arguments and asking probing questions as two important critical thinking skills. Constructing logical arguments requires students to provide reasons, evidence and conclusions. Students must explain their positions, provide evidence, and determine what to do with the information. Reflective responses are one way to provide students with practice in constructing logical arguments. They must summarize the material, explain the impact on them using evidence from the material, and describe the relevance to the reader. When sharing responses with classmates, they ask probing questions of one another.

Making Connections

With reflective responses, students make connections. They connect what they already know to what they are learning. They connect past experiences to new experiences. They connect information across classes. Students are active participants. Two examples of ways in which students can make connections are field experiences and responses to current stories in the media.

Field Experience Reflection

"Critical reflection is the process of analyzing, reconsidering, and questioning one's experiences within a broad context of issued and content knowledge" (Jacoby, 2015, p. 26). Identified as an important component of service learning, critical reflection can be applied to any experiential learning. It should occur before, during, and after experiences and allow students to make connections between theory and practice (Jacoby, 2015). Students participate in the field in a meaningful way. This participation could include volunteering, classroom observation, job shadowing, or participating in community events. Ideally, this activity occurs throughout the semester, but a field experience reflection can also occur with a one-time event. In field experience reflections students summarize what happened, explain how it differs from previous experiences, explain what they found surprising, and provide some evidence from their course readings or other materials. One way to share field experience reflections is online on the discussion board. Students can both make connections between their experiences and those of their peers.

Current News Story Response

Students learn to monitor their own understanding with reflective responses (Nilson, 2013). Using the "What, So what, Now What?" model provides a useful framework for reflection (Jacoby, 2015, p. 49). Using this model, the student can employ a current news story related to class content as a case study of sorts. First, students share "What?" this issue is. Whether reading an article or watching a video, students can explain what the story was about. In response to the question "So What?" they can describe why the article is important using course resources or other resources for evidence. Finally, "Now what?" involves application, reflecting on how the information can be used either currently or in their prospective professions. Sharing reflections with peers in class allows students to ask each other probing questions and receive feedback beyond that of the course instructor.

Conclusion

Ultimately, the goal is that anytime you assign material for students to read or view, you also provide an opportunity to probe, process, and respond to that work. It should not be busy work however; it should be intentional meaning-making work. Students should be aware of its purpose and engaged by it as well. Students should not be asking the questions, "Why is this important?" and "When am I ever going to use this?" They should be answering those questions themselves. In responding to these questions, they are thinking critically about the materials and experiences provided in and out of class.

References

Downing, S. (2017). On course: *Strategies for creating success in college and life study skills plus* (3rd ed). Boston, MA: Cengage.

Jacoby, B. (2015). *Service-learning essentials: Questions, answers and lessons learned.* San Francisco, CA: Jossey- Bass.

Nilson, L.B. (2013). *Creating self- regulated learners: Strategies to strengthen students' self-awareness and learning skills.* Sterling, VA: Stylus.

Helene Arbouet Harte, Ed.D., University of Cincinnati – Blue Ash College

Understanding Ethos in the Public Speaking Classroom

The Public Speaking classroom provides a stage where the college rhetorician learns the art of persuasion through oral delivery. Aristotle, the father of oral rhetoric, emphasizes "that the speaker's ethos is the most potent of all means to persuasion" (Cooper, 1930, p. 9). So, it is vital that the college student is able to define and then determine the components of ethos that are required for his or her success. When the students enter the classroom, they are concerned about their own ethos – how to get through the class and get an A. However, the following strategy will challenge the self-centered approach to ethos and help students discover the importance of a collective ethos that will drive their success.

Ethos

So, what is ethos and how is it related to delivering an effective speech? These two questions lay the foundation for further discussion as the students ponder the importance of credibility within public speaking. During the first speech, the spotlight is on them. This introduction speech allows the student to share strategic information with the rest of the class, but in so doing, the student is also establishing some credibility while learning to master the orator's art. The first step in understanding the importance of ethos involves self-discovery. Students must see where they need to improve and why it is important for them to speak with conviction.

Ethos can be simply defined as credibility. College students entering a Public Speaking class for the first time are concerned about how they can build their own credibility as an effective presenter while managing their nerves and remembering the material. The camera, of sorts, is on them, and they listen to lectures, read the textbook, and interact with their classmates with the desire to find the key to developing an approach to public speaking that will foster success.

Basic Technique

The first stage in fostering students' critical thinking in relation to ethos is about basic techniques. Voice inflection, hand movements, and eye contact are a few of the many skills that need to be assessed and improved upon so that the student's performance is not distracting. However, to move students to further develop their critical thinking skills, we need to ask them, "What gives you confidence when you are presenting?" The answer is ethos, but it is not just about the delivery of the information, it is about the authority that comes with the delivery.

Select a short speech of an impressive speaker, and have students critically examine what makes that speaker appear confident. At first the techniques used in the delivery will be identified, but have the students move the discussion to content and the power of the message.

Necessary Content

Now that the students have an appreciation for technique, it is time to move their focus to the content. Ethos within rhetoric is defined by Hyde (2008) as a "principled self that instructs the moral consciousness and actions of others and thereby serves as a possible catalyst for them to do the same" (abstract). The message has to move the audience, and that movement begins with students selecting a motivating topic they believe in – a topic they can confidently talk about.

In small groups, have students discuss if they are an authority on anything and then have them each identify at least one thing. Next, have them discuss what makes them an authority. Bring the students together to share their answers and help them to discover their hesitancy to claim to be an authority. This action will begin their realization that credibility is fortified by sources outside themselves.

Critical Sources

A speech is as good as its sources. This is the conclusion you want students to reach, but they need to carefully consider what it takes to reach this conclusion. In order to help them reach this conclusion, choose a controversial topic and present it to the class. Then, make a controversial statement regarding the topic that clearly takes a side and ask the class to react. Defend your position as your own authority. Move the class to recognize that your authority (even as the instructor) is not enough. Guide the discussion so that you illicit a response that helps students see the need for research to be a part of the defense.

When students understand the value of research, they will quickly discover the rhetorical influence being added to their growing ethos as a public speaker. This confidence not only brings added strength to their message, but it also gives them confidence in the actual delivery. When students have something important to say and the integrity of the message is supported by reliable research, then the focus is off the performance and on the message.

Conclusion

In order to help students develop critical thinking skills in the Public Speaking course, the instructor must first address the techniques. However, it is critical that students transition to content and the importance of the message over the delivery. Finally, when students embrace a strengthened ethos resulting from research, they will more fully understand the power that can be theirs as an oral rhetorician.

References

Cooper, L. (1930). *The rhetoric of Aristotle.* New York, NY: D. Appleton.

Hyde, M.J. (2008). Ethos and rhetoric. *The International Encyclopedia of Communication.* Retrieved from https://onlinelibrary.wiley.com/doi/abs/10.1002/9781405186407wbiece043.pub2

Dr. Mary-Lynn Chambers, Elizabeth City State University

Let's Have a Discussion

I am sure we can all think back to a class discussion that inspired us to continue processing the topic long after the class ended. Class debates, small group debates, class dialogue, small group dialogue, think-pair-share, and online class forums are all examples of how active discussion can be used to foster critical thinking. This idea that discussion facilitates critical thinking is not revolutionary. Rather, it dates back to the Socratic method, in which the goal is to explore and clarify concepts through dialogue and questioning (Abrami, Bernard, Borokhovski, Waddington, Wade, & Persson, 2015).

Discussion facilitates critical thinking when individuals process many facets of a topic together. This processing can occur through question asking, dialogue, or debate. Encouraging students to voice their thoughts and ideas with one another often forces them to consider alternative opinions or perspectives. Group discussion also promotes teamwork and interpersonal skills, given that expressing agreement, and especially disagreement, can require finesse.

As mentioned earlier, discussion can take many different forms, involving myriad techniques. Each of these discussion techniques is helpful; however, the most effective of improving critical thinking occurs when the instructor asks the questions. Specifically, critical thinking skills are fostered when the instructor leads the entire class in discussion and facilitates small group discussions (Abrami et al., 2015). A teacher-facilitated discussion is more likely to hold the attention of students and encourage them to engage their critical thinking skills, as asking thought-provoking questions and promoting participation is modeled.

However, it is easy for class discussion to become unruly, resulting in students going off topic, talking amongst themselves, or becoming disrespectful to peers. This disruption is especially possible during debates or questions considering controversial issues, which can become heated quickly.

Three techniques can be useful in managing classroom discussions.

First, as instructors, we need to be involved in the dialogue. This engagement is a balancing act though. We need to be comfortable correcting misunderstandings and steering the conversation in the desired direction. Asking specific questions that challenge students to consider an alternative perspective is critical. Similarly, challenging students when they fail to adequately evaluate evidence is important.

Second, discussions need ground rules. Discussion in any course should be civil; students need to be respectful of varying opinions but appropriately assertive in expressing their side of any argument. Many instructors prefer to develop discussion rules on their own, sharing them with their students. Another option is for the instructor to develop discussion rules in concert with students.

Finally, it's up to the instructor to ensure that all students participate in class discussion. It's easy to have a "class" discussion devolve into a heated exchange between a small group of students. Although both the instructor and this small subset of students may walk away with the impression that the discussion was exhilarating, the remainder of the students may be bored. Numerous options are available to resolve this dilemma. Some instructors prefer calling on all students in a systematized manner. Others prefer allowing students to engage in a modified think-pair-share. Finally, instructors may assign students to small groups for discussion prior to having groups share their thoughts with the entire class.

Overall, class discussion can be a wonderful technique to assess students' knowledge and understanding of course topics, their ability to apply this understanding to hypothetical situations, and their ability to respond appropriately and engage with other students. When utilized to its fullest, class discussion and debate facilitates the use of critical thinking skills and promotes an atmosphere of learning and mutual respect for the thoughts and opinions of others. Odds are, if you are like us, you will also very likely learn something from your students as you stay involved in the discussion.

References

Abrami, P. C., Bernard, R. M., Borokhovski, E., Waddington, D. I., Wade, C. E., & Persson, T. (2015). Strategies for teaching students to think critically: A meta-analysis. *Review of Educational Research, 85*(2). 275-314. doi: 10.3102/0034654314551063

Anna Grace Cooper, Spalding University
Robin Morgan, Indiana University Southeast
Nate Mitchell, Spalding University

If You Can Teach It, You Probably Are Thinking Critically About It

If we are to be completely honest, many student presentations are lack-luster at best. Fellow students very often complain about the boredom-inducing presentations of their fellow students. Additionally, many students assume student presentations are a means by which instructors avoid working. And, to be fair, many times these student reactions are valid. However, if done with a high degree of thoughtfulness, student led class *facilitations* (not presentations), can be a powerful tool for developing critical thinking of both the student(s) conducting the facilitation and their peers.

One strategy for modifying the traditional "student presentation" to enhance critical thinking works well with advanced undergraduate or graduate students. First, we changed the name of the assignment from class presentation to *class facilitation*. In doing so, we explain that we do not want students lecturing to the class by reading a PowerPoint. In contrast, we expect students to develop a short lesson plan with the express purpose of increasing their peers' critical thinking about a given topic. Students are asked to research effective classroom activities to promote critical thinking, determine which activity might best be incorporated with their content assignment, and then create a lesson plan. Students then submit their lesson plan two weeks prior to their scheduled facilitation, allowing for the instructor to fine-tune the plan when necessary.

Clearly, this activity works best when used with more advanced students. The first author (NM) trains doctoral students in a professional psychology program. Linking this assignment to their future work has been helpful in getting students out of the previous "boring student presentation" modality by asking them to consider the task as a "mini-workshop facilitation." Students are asked, what would make you WANT to attend a workshop from a particular facilitator? Further, students are asked to consider some of the most helpful/interesting/critical thinking enhancing classes or workshops they've attended and what were the elements that promoted such a learning experience? (Honestly, NM is secretly hoping they talk about some of his classes and/or workshops as examples, but this doesn't always happen!).

Students often need support and guidance for this novel and complex assignment. First, we provide a detailed rubric with a particular emphasis on the student(s)' ability to promote critical thinking through both providing novel information beyond required readings and the development of a minimum of one active/problem-based learning activity. Second, we provide them with common SoTL sources where they can learn more about effective classroom activities to promote critical thinking (e.g., the *It Works for Me* series!). Third, we provide feedback on the proposed lesson plan well in advance of the facilitation. Doing so allows the students to have time to make any necessary/recommended changes, and also allows us to ensure we do not duplicate any of the activities or content the student(s) is choosing to cover. Fourth, we provide copious handwritten feedback during the facilitation on the rubric. Doing so allows students to have detailed, thoughtful, and immediate feedback concerning their hard work.

To date, the student feedback on the *facilitations* have been overwhelmingly positive! Students report they prefer the *facilitation* approach over the traditional student presentation. Even more gratifying is that students are more successful in achieving learning outcomes using this strategy.

One of the co-authors of this article (AGC) was previously a student in one of the first author's (NM) classes and was required to develop a *facilitation*. She provided the following feedback concerning the assignment:

"There have been a few classes when I have been required to teach or facilitate the class. These assignments were the ones from which I learned the most, as I have to express a level of understanding of the material in order to teach it to the class. These assignments required me to critically think about how to apply the material, rather than just memorize it. They required me to be creative when devising activities that would engage the class in the learning process."

Nate Mitchell, Spalding University
Robin Morgan, Indiana University Southeast
Anna Grace Cooper, Spalding University

Embracing the Dark Side: Playing the Bad Guy in an Education Environment

Overview

The notion that teachers should encourage a "positive teaching environment" (PTE) seems to be universally accepted as a strategy that educators should strive for in the classroom. One method of teaching that is often avoided is creating a negative teaching environment or playing the bad guy. This practical pretending/role playing model introduces negative issues that must be addressed for positive outcomes. Students are often familiar with the concepts, such as opposing viewpoints, cause & effect, debate analysis, but they are rarely engaged in a practical, real-life environment where they must deal opposing viewpoints. This bad guy teaching method forces students to use critical thinking skills to positively succeed.

In many social situations, the average person will be required to interact with people in different power positions, such as bosses, spouses, customers, politicians, or drill sergeants. Social interactions are not always positive and comfortable. The skills to manage unpleasant interactions at an individual level or to endure unpleasant interactions should be addressed, taught, or practiced in the classroom setting.

Implementation

How do you implement this concept in the classroom? Constant opportunities exist, but the instructor would want to optimize the best exercise for maximum results. In English the instructor can be a boss and provide a set of objectives that need to be carried out before the class is over. Students may need to conduct research to meet their objectives. They will definitely have to prepare some type of written document. Service Learning and Experiential Learning exercises provide opportunities for working with organizations where hierarchies must be respected, and rules understood and followed.

Employers

How many jobs have you had where the focus was on the employee? Usually, the focus is on the customer or the boss. When you get hired as a new employee, you are often a tool to complete certain tasks. You cannot pick and choose what you will or won't do. The focus is not on you, rather the objectives set by the boss.

An employee may be referred to a team player. You must get on-board. You must conform. You must do what you are told. The team players perspective should be—it is not about me. It is about my superiors. It is about moving the organization forward regardless of the individual employee's perspective.

Customers

Most people have heard the phrase, "The customer is always right." Obviously, it is not always true. How did this phrase come about? It came about because the focus was on the customer and not the employees. The truth of the matter is that the customer is not always right, but you must manage the emotions of the customer so as to not negatively affect the bottom-line. Otherwise, you may hurt their feelings, embarrass them, or make them feel inferior, causing customers to take their business somewhere else.

Politicians

Politicians are notorious for giving a passionate description of their perspectives and a pithy attack on their opponent. To really understand the issues, everyone should be fully aware of both sides of an issue before making any conclusions. However, most people do not have the time, patience or even research skills to find out the opposing viewpoints.

Truth, knowledge, and facts are not always the center of a discussion. Emotions, bias and tradition may trump any other information. The average individual may not want to hear or accept any other viewpoint than their own. The well-informed, balanced attitude, and truth-seeking individual will take the time to seek out the truth, logic, and credible information and experts.

Drill Sergeants

Anyone who as ever gone into the military can usually, vividly recall their drill sergeant. The objectives and goals of the training are clearly established, and the recruit must fall right into place. Falling into place usually means attitude, behavior, and even dress code. The easiest way to survive basic training is to play by their rules. Rebelling against the system will bring down the wrath of the drill sergeants.

Conclusion

Most of the concepts mentioned appear to be negative, but they don't have to be. In fact, strengthening your viewpoint should be a positive experience. Getting along with your boss or a teacher should also be the norm. One of the greatest activities for many people is playing sports. For every sport you have an enemy. In most cases you have a timed enemy—when the clock runs out, they are no longer your opponent. Often when a Pee Wee Hockey or Pop Warner Youth Football game is over, they have the children shake each other's hands.

Even in adult games the opposing players often congratulate or provide condolences with the other players. They might even quickly analyze the highlights (or low points) of the game. Even in the locker room there might be a debriefing on the strategies, actions, and circumstances of the game. For the most part there is a mutual respect for the opposing players. It is the opposing player who forces you to "up-your-game" and become better. It is the opposing players that make you evaluate yourself. It is the opposing player who may even make you see the worst in yourself and force you to make changes. Examining opposing players or opponents—or the dark side—is an essential part to learning, growing and evolving. This concept was clearly understood by the Jedi Master in Star Wars.

> "Yoda wisely knows that fear, anger, hate, and aggression lead to suffering and the Dark Side of the Force, and his wisdom allows him to tell the difference between the Light Side and the Dark Side of the Force. Yoda explains to Luke that he will know the difference between the two when he is "calm, at peace, passive." (Stephens 2005)

References

Stephens, W. O. (2005). Stoicism in the stars: Yoda, the Emperor, and the Force. In *Star Wars and Philosophy: More Powerful than You Can Possibly Imagine*. Popular Culture and Philosphy. Edited by Kevin S. Decker, Jason T. Eberl, and William Irwin. Open Court: Chicago, Illinois.

Tim Hibsman, Indiana University of Pennsylvania
Lydia Rose, Kent State University

IV. Assignments and Exercises: An Overview

While developing theoretical approaches and creating effective strategies for fostering critical thinking in your students are important, perhaps no area fits our *It Works for Me* series better than those day-to-day assignments and exercises designed to enhance students' skills through application. In the following essays, you will find suggestions for incorporating such interactive techniques as debates, "essential questions," relevant news stories, role playing, "dirty writing," and "walking on eggs." Other essays detail the use of technology, such as photography, mobile phones, and video production. Moreover, you'll find assignments and exercises appropriate for on-ground and/or on-line classes.

Use the materials as they appear, or tailor them to meet your specific needs—whatever works for you.

Technology to Enhance Preservice Teachers' Critical Thinking

One of the essential goals in training future teachers is to help them develop both lower-level and higher-level critical thinking skills. These skills include students' ability to conceptualize, analyze, synthesize, evaluate new information and connect it to previous knowledge, as well as solve problems systematically. The need for such skills encouraged the International Society for Technology in Education (ISTE), the largest community of global educators, to adopt critical thinking skills as one of its standards for teachers. Furthermore, critical thinking became an integral part for training preservice teachers to effectively diffuse technology in future classrooms. Therefore, technology and critical thinking are essential elements for teacher preparation programs and students' success in the 21st century classroom.

The integration of technology in my daily classroom activities through hands-on and project-based coursework helped my students to achieve two goals, implementing the course learning objectives and gaining critical thinking skills. The classroom activities include the use of a wide variety of technology tools to produce personalized artifacts, apply knowledge in real-world contexts, engage in higher-level thinking, collaborate with classmates, and encourage the expression of diverse opinions. An example of the use of technology in my class activities and its positive effect on students' critical thinking skills can be demonstrated by a video class project. In this project, the task was to create a short digital video about lessons students will teach in their future classroom using a free video web tool to edit and publish online. Students were free to choose an online video editing tool such as WeVideo, Animoto, PowToon, or any other tool they preferred, or had access to. The project aimed to include several critical thinking skills, such as searching for the information they would present, developing a cohesive script based on the information they learned and collected, planning the video production steps, creating the final video lesson, commenting and providing feedback on classmates' videos.

In the first step of this technology project, students were to prepare their own script and storyboard following the class writing conventions. The scripts were developed based on the course learning materials and the information that students searched and collected on the presented topic. Students also spent adequate time to watch other online video examples to explore different ideas or to learn other effective video techniques.

During the script writing process, students considered the suitability of the information to their audience. After writing the script and storyboard, they had to practice speaking and presenting their information with confidence and for varied audience in attractive and effective way, including activating prior knowledge and giving a purpose to the video message. Therefore, students spent time to practice their talk on camera to make sure they looked knowledgeable in the subject through the information presented, their dress, actions, and body language. I found that the script writing process helped students to improve their research and writing skills as well as practicing their communication knowledge. This assignment was also a great way to assess how well students understood the information and concepts covered in the course.

For the video post-production process, students had to use multimedia, such as images, audio, personal narratives, video, effective graphics, record of a presentation, or capture a screencast element. Students were encouraged to use these video production elements by applying the principles of universal design for learning (UDL) to consider the differences among the viewers. The use of the multimedia in educational video is supported by large body of research that indicates that multimedia not only help to clarify complex concepts and procedures through presenting the message in multiple formats, but also stimulate the viewers and improve the delivered message. Furthermore, according to Mayer's cognitive theory of multimedia learning (CTML), presenting the information using words and pictures is better than words alone. Consequently, students had to consider using multimedia in their final video based on the design principles of Mayer's theory and the UDL. Encouraging students to consider these design principles while developing the video project helped them to develop important design-thinking skills, building positive digital footprints and learning digital literacy skills.

The final video was then presented by students in the classroom. While the main purpose for students' presentations was to share their teaching videos with their classmates, the project also provided an excellent opportunity to reinforce their essential presentation skills, to get acquainted with the components of public speaking, and to overcome the performance anxiety. To prepare for their speech, each student developed an online presentation using one of the free web tools such as Google Slides, Prezi, Zoho Show, Emaze, FlowVella or any other tool they preferred. The online presentation helped students to use a written outline to present their work, give a clear and structured order to the information they were offering and share the presentation link with their audience. After students' presentations, they were instructed to provide detailed feedback on two of their classmates' videos presentations using a class rubric. Students' feedback included detailed comment on two of their peers' video design, its message, special effects, and the recorded voice. Students' reflections on their peers' videos was a great platform for students to promote an open discussion, hear different perspectives, demonstrate communication skills with their peers, and encourage class debate and the reflection on the topics presented to assess the learning objectives.

This classroom exercise is an example of how technology-rich activities can transform a class assignment into a meaningful learning experience and result in rich critical thinking. The sequence of the video production activity offered a learning platform engaging students completely with class work both cognitively and emotionally. Each step of the project prompted students to engage with the learning content and foster self-regulated learning, regardless of their learning styles. Students' also experienced the process of complex learning through the constant connection between knowledge acquired from the current assignment to previous learnings materials (scaffolding). Finally, the video project, presentation, and the peer feedback activities helped students to engage in practical skills through deliberate and systematic critical thinking and deep learning activities whereby they learned how to apply these skills successfully in their future classroom.

Mohamed Ibrahim, Arkansas Tech University

To Write Dirty, You Have to Know What Clean Is

Sometimes it is just more fun to be dirty rather than clean. That is the premise for one of my in-class review activities in our sophomore-level Advanced Programming course, but I bet it can be adapted for any subject. A major focus of this particular course is having the students learn, recognize, and successfully produce clean code using test-driven development. We use Martin's *Clean Code* (2009) as our primary student resource. This book describes an in-depth, but easy to follow set of principles and guidelines, which, if followed, helps guarantee the code you write is clean. Clean code is generally considered to be easy to be read and understood by others and has an elegance to it.

In this course, we spend the first four weeks focused on the individual student, and it is during this time that all reading assignments from the book are given. I use a series of six small assignments that have them review their past code and make observations about why it should not be considered clean. The remainder of the semester has the students create larger and larger projects, first in pairs, and then in groups of three or four students. The intent is to get them familiar with clean code and test-driven development during the first month and then have them progressively apply what they have learned during the rest of the semester when developing larger projects.

At the end of the first four weeks, I announce the aforementioned in-class clean code review activity. (I suspect it would work as a homework assignment as well, but I like to interact with the students while they develop their solutions.) I present it in the context of them having spent a month learning about clean code; now let's see how well they can implement it in class while working with two or three other students. I tell them to form small groups, to get their computers out, and that they have thirty minutes to accomplish this activity. I then display the following on the screen.

Create a program which will accomplish the following:
- Conversion between any combination of
  - Fahrenheit
  - Celsius
  - Kelvin
- Calculation of Wind Chill, if you have time
- The code must generate correct answers
- The code must be as "dirty" as possible.

I usually start to hear a few mummers and chuckles around the room as students get to the last statement in the activity instructions. Inevitably, someone asks what I mean, and I simply reply that I want them to break as many of the clean code principles as possible, thus writing dirty code. At that point, the room usually becomes a flurry of activity as the groups try to get organized and figure out how they're going to accomplish this task placed before them. Few, if any, know the conversion formulas, so some are looking on the web for them. Others are starting to piece together the outline of the code. Ultimately, it starts coming together for most groups, and they start making significant progress.

Once the groups have a good start, I wander around the room to help them make their code dirtier. Usually, after four weeks of my having drilled into their head "variable names must be descriptive," they're using very descriptive variable names in their code. I ask them why, and usually get a blank expression back from the group, indicating that they are confused about why I don't want them to use descriptive names. Then it dawns on someone what they've done, and suddenly the name of the variable destined to hold the Fahrenheit temperature changes from "fahrenheitTemperature" to "f", or, even better, simply the letter "a". A few more questions from me to other groups, and the code starts to truly look awful, which is a good thing.

After the thirty minutes have elapsed, I ask who believes they have the dirtiest code and proceed to show a few of their examples on the screen for the rest of the class to see. I ask each presenting group to highlight the clean code principles they've violated. Afterwards, I facilitate a debriefing with the students, exploring what they just experienced. They usually don't realize until this activity how much they've actually learned, and how much cleaner their code has become over the last month. Some observe that their code from this activity looks like what they'd have written before starting the semester and are a bit embarrassed to admit they used to write code that dirty.

Someone usually asks (and if they don't, I do) why I have them try to write the dirtiest code rather than the cleanest code for this activity. My reasons are twofold. First, it seems to produce a friendlier competition to write dirty code. People sometimes become rather defensive trying to justify why their code is the cleanest; not so much about the dirtiest. It just becomes a fun activity to see how bad they can do it. Secondly, I figure the more principles you can knowingly violate, the better you know the principles. Since they're working in small groups, this activity becomes an opportunity for students to grasp a principle they had not yet understood, but another student has. It also provides me insight about the students' collective understanding of the clean code principles.

If we define critical thinking as applying knowledge, then I've had the students do that in this fun activity, perhaps without them even realizing it. As they develop their solution, they are thinking about what is needed to accomplish the task, and how they can do it wrong, but still produce the correct results. Groups often mention it was easier to write clean code for the activity and then make it dirty afterwards, demonstrating they have learned one of the key benefits of clean code. A bit of critical thinking applied in just the right way can lead to some great dirty fun.

Reference

Martin, R. C. (2009). *Clean code: A Handbook of agile software craftsmanship*. New York, NY: Prentice Hall.

David L. Largent, Ball State University

Extending the Thinking of Preservice Early Childhood Educators through Creative Application

High-Impact Practice Addressed: Collaborative Assignments and Projects

As part of their teacher preparation program, preservice early childhood educators (PECE) are required to take a course called *Introduction to Child Development*. This foundational survey course introduces PECE to the basic theories related to the growth and development of children prenatally through age 8. The course covers all of the developmental domains, including physical, fine and gross motor, cognitive, language, social, and emotional development; it presents theorists such as Piaget, Vygotsky, Bronfenbrunner, Erikson, Skinner, and Bandura and explores the basic tenets of the many developmental theories introduced.

In order to ensure that the PECE have met the learning outcomes for the course, they are required to observe a child between the birth and age 8, taking observational field notes while watching their child in naturalistic settings. Using their field notes, students apply the concepts and vocabulary introduced in class to the information garnered during the observation. In order to illustrate their mastery of both the course content and observational techniques, the PECE write three cohesive synthesis papers wherein they determine and explore the relative developmental strengths and weakness of their target child with regard to all six of the domains. In essence, they must determine if the child's development is typical or atypical, provide evidence from their field observation log, and cite appropriate research and theory to support their determination.

The synthesis papers are useful in my assessment of the PECE's level of understanding of developmental theory, the efficiency of their field observational practice, and their overall ability to evaluate students' words and behavior in the field. However, the papers alone do not tell me what the PECE, who are moving toward teaching as their career goal, understand about those assessments and how they will translate into pedagogical practice in the early childhood classroom. For this reason, I recently added the "theme box project" that allows PECE to extend their thinking about students' developmental strengths and weaknesses and connect it to future evaluative teacher behavior and classroom praxis planning.

The "theme box project" requires the PECE to look at all that they have learned about their target child from a holistic perspective and to design, based on their evaluations, an educational tool for the child's use. The PECE are required to obtain and decorate a small "toy" chest that can hold at least five items. The child will use these items independently or in collaboration with an adult for the purpose of improving, developing, or extending skills in each of the domains.

As the name implies, the box must be themed (e.g., insects, princesses, Iron Man, *Moana*, etc.) and the five items included in the box should be consistent with that theme. Each of the items that are in the box should review, practice, extend, or encourage knowledge or skill development that is appropriate for the particular child. One or more of the activities must represent each of the domain areas (physical/motor, social/emotional, cognitive /language). In order to ensure connections between theory and practice, the PECE must submit a typewritten paper that explains what each item is, how it will be used by or with the child, what areas of development are targeted by the item, and what is known about the child that warrants its use.

The boxes that have been developed represent a wide range of interest and level of involvement between the PECE and the target child. Boxes have used decorated shoe boxes with or without lids, baskets, buckets, small plastic totes, and even a handmade wooden "pirate chest." Through this project, the PECE exemplify not only an understanding of their target child's interests and hobbies, but being able to apply their burgeoning understanding of the sequence of abilities and knowledge, in addition to developmental milestones.

For example, one PECE developed a theme box for a six-year-old girl named Delaney that she entitled, *Girls Night In*. The PECE chose this theme because "the six-year-old I observed is a girly girl and loves doing very hands-on stuff with her friends." The five items she chose were nail polish, cards, a speaker, crayons/ sparkly gel paint, and a measuring cup. According to the PECE's narrative, the nail polish focuses on "fine motor skills, eye-hand coordination, and finger dexterity. While polishing nails, Delaney has to focus on using her smaller muscles to keep the paint on the toenails and avoid the skin." The playing cards were included because "playing cards are beneficial to a six-year-old because they help with cognitive thinking and development. Playing cards can also offer social enjoyment and friendly competition." The third prop, a speaker, represents music or a dance party. "Dancing uses gross motor skills that help improve balance, coordination, strength and knowing where one's body is in space." The fourth prop was crayons and sparkling glitter pens "because Delaney is always creating artwork to give to her friends and family... Some benefits to arts and crafts are they help improve fine motor coordination, they help with self-regulation, crafts are a self-esteem booster, and they allow bonding and fun! These are all categories of emotional and social development that can help benefit a child around Delaney's age." The final item was a measuring cup, representing baking because baking "can help with social and emotional development. It can help develop pride and confidence in their own skills and abilities, and the act of following a recipe can encourage self-direction and independence, while also teaching children to follow directions and use thinking skills to problem solve. Cooking is a great opportunity for language development and learning new words and also promotes cognitive and motor development." This PECE ends by stating, "I feel this will help Delaney learn to her fullest. My box fits Delaney's personality perfectly and I just know she'll love to open it when I present it to her."

Through this project, the PECE illustrate not only their understanding of what their target child enjoyed, but also what skills and activities were age- and developmentally-appropriate. While some pre-service teacher candidates purchased an item or two for their boxes, most created the materials themselves.

Angela M. Miller-Hargis, University of Cincinnati Blue Ash

Classroom Mobiling: A Critical Thinking Exercise for the Millennial Student

Many college teachers today have realized the challenges of trying to motivate, connect with, and actively engage their students. For example, today's Millennial student will often "tune out" any college teacher who relies too heavily on traditional classroom lecture. They often learn more effectively when interacting with teachers in different ways other than lecture to gain subject matter knowledge (Kotz, 2016, McGlynn, 2012). McGlynn (2012) claims a paradigm shift began in the 1990's in traditional undergraduate education with a new focus on what the college learner is doing in class rather than on what the instructor is doing and "covering" in traditional lecture formats. Doing is more important than knowing for the Millennial student (Northern, n.d.).

Research also indicate that Millennial students expect to talk more in the classroom and seek engaging creative experiences where they learn, using technology while interacting with others in small group settings (Kotz 2016, McGlynn, 2007, Monaco & Martin 2007). They have a short attention span and value interaction and approachability with their teachers versus subject matter knowledge (Price, n.d.). They also enjoy being part of "learning communities" in a classroom setting where they can discuss and analyze together different readings and assignments related to important class topics (Kotz, 2016). Millennial students also desire to become more intentional architects of their own learning and enjoy exploring, reflecting, and integrating acquired knowledge into their existing worldviews (Crone & Mackay, 2007).

Previous research indicates today's college student requires different methodologies and methods to help facilitate development of their skills in critical thinking. Critical thinking is different from both analytical and lateral thinking by encouraging students to make judgments on data/information that is free from false premises or bias (Watanabe-Crockett, 2017). In this article, I will discuss a classroom exercise named "Classroom Mobiling" that I use with my students as a method to encourage development of their critical thinking skills. This exercise involves the teacher asking students to use their smart phone, IPad, tablet or laptop technology they bring to class to do online research related to a learning topic being discussed. Below, I will briefly discuss four simple steps to implement "Classroom Mobiling" with students:

1. During lecture, ask students to retrieve their mobile technology, go online, and individually conduct a search process using Google, Chrome, or some other search engine service to explore what they learn on a classroom topic, or answer a question related to that topic. What new information can they learn related to this topic? How does this information relate to text learning on the term or question? What are the sources for this information? Do they agree/disagree with this information? Why? Questions such as these are what you may ask students to reflect on after they conduct their individual online search.
2. Students should be given 5-7 minutes to individually explore different search sites they find.
3. At the end of the time period, place students in pairs and ask them to share with each other what they have learned from their online search. Encourage the student pairs to attempt to come to consensus of insights about the term or question.
4. Ask for volunteers to share the results of their online search process with all students in the class. While they are sharing results, write on the whiteboard key points of this search process so that all students in the class can reflect on a summary of these different shared research insights related to a term or topic question.

I have found use of Classroom Mobiling to be a very helpful approach to "break up" the traditional lecture format and generate more interest in learning with my students. Classroom Mobiling teaches students to incorporate their personal use of mobile technology in interactive ways that lead to more active learning and development of their skill in critical thinking. They learn more about becoming a critical thinker by "doing" than by passively listening to a lecture from a teacher. Today's students crave personal choice and enjoy the opportunity to explore and learn on their own. Students also enjoy the opportunity to work in small and large groups and share their learning with others.

References

Crone, I, & Mackay, K. (2007). Motivating today's college students. *Association of American Colleges & Universities, 9*(1), 18-22.

Gazdecki, A. (2018). How teachers can leverage mobile in the classroom. *Bizness Apps.* Retrieved from https://www.biznessapps.com/blog/mobile-in-the-classroom/

Kotz, P.E. (2016). Reaching the millennial generation in the classroom. *Universal Journal of Educational Research 4*(5), 1163-1166. doi: 10.13189/ujer.2016. 040528

McGlynn, A.P. (2007). Millennials in college: How do we motivate them? *Hispanic Outlook in Higher Education, 17,* 34-34.

McGlynn, A.P. (2012). *Motivating today's college students: The millennial generation.* Prezi.com. Retrieved from https://prezi.com/ephqeviwoaf/motivating-todays-college-students-the-millennial-generation/

Monaco, M & Martin, M (2007). The millennial student: A new generation of learners. *Athletic Training Education Journal: 2*(Apr-Jun), 42-46.

Northern Illinois University. (n.d.). Faculty Development and Instructional Design Center. Retrieved from facdev@niu.edu.www.niu.edu/facdev.

Price, C. (n.d.). *Motivate, engage and inspire: Tips for teaching modern learners.* Madison, WI: Magna. Retrieved from https://www.magnapus.com (online seminars).

Watanabe-Crockett, L. (2017). *Here are some critical thinking exercises that will blow your learners' minds.* Retrieved from https://globaldigitalcitizen.org/critical-thinking-exercises-blow-students-minds

Breck A. Harris, Fresno Pacific University

Using Students' Career Dreams to Think and Research Outside the Box

This tip is about how writing and research instructors collaborated using critical thinking to compose an assignment challenging students to think critically. While the classroom instructor had doubts about whether students would rise to the challenge, the resulting essays projected the voices of the writers. These Generation Z students found the task intrinsically motivating. As one wrote, "It's important to think about your career because you can't reach a goal that was never made."

Setting Up Students for Success

To begin the ENG 102 Writing, Rhetoric, and Research course, Gaby wanted an assignment that encouraged critical thinking and oral research. Thus, the Prompt for Essay 1 was to "choose someone you know very well who holds a strong opinion with which you differ. Explain how their background, experiences, and circumstances have shaped their opinion. Your rhetorical purpose is to persuade us that you understand and empathize with the individual." She encouraged students to engage with friends, family, and other acquaintances for reliable sources.

Visualize	*Five years from now, I will be an outstanding _____* [fill in your job title upon graduation].
Remember	Begin a sentence with one of the following prompts: *I first realized I wanted to be a...when...* *When...happened, I knew I was going to...* *From the moment I met..., I knew I wanted to be a...*
Explode the Sentence	*Five years from now, I will be an outstanding* [fill in your first job title]. Explain what traits you possess that will make you a good fit for your dream job.

Figure 1: Getting Started on Essay 2

As with their first essay, she recommended students integrate their ideas with the ideas of others to build their argument, suggesting parents, teachers, and friends as trustworthy sources.

Developing the Researched Essay Assignment

For Essay 3, Gaby asked to collaborate with Karen to come up with a topic related to students' careers for their final research essay. Karen thought outside the box, suggesting students compile a mini portfolio of career information sources and rate their quality and credibility.

Gaby solicited help developing a prompt for Essay 3 because she wanted to avoid a prompt that would lead to job reports. To encourage critical thinking, Karen suggested telling students that we expected more than reportage and would put more grade emphasis on their personal self-evaluations and reflections.

The Assignment

Write a researched essay in which you engage in personal self-evaluation and reflection on the following questions about your target career field. Note that the questions cover three separate points in time. As Essay 2 touched on the "Now," I am especially interested in your look ahead.

Now
- At present, how well do you match up with the attributes required in your target field?
- Do you find any areas/traits/skills that you are lacking? What might you plan to do to remedy these issues? Are any of these issues insurmountable due to personal preferences, expense, etc.?
- What kinds of work experiences or internships would help position you for your first job in your target field?

At 30 years old
- Looking ahead to a career progression in your target field, what might you expect to be doing in ten years?
- What is the significance of the work you have chosen on the people living around you? How will your work in the target field impact where you are living in Kentucky or elsewhere?

At 60 years old
- Based on these long-term career expectations, when the day comes that you retire, what will you be especially proud of in terms of your own accomplishments, providing for your family, setting an example to youth, providing a service to your community?
- What else might be especially meaningful about what you have spent most of your life doing?

Figure 2: Prompt for Essay 3

Doing Research

Since Essay 3 asked students to expand and extrapolate from Essay 2, the challenge for this assignment was to reflect on their career dreams, place them in the context of their life dreams, and research their options with faculty advisors and professionals in their chosen field. Two library instruction sessions led them to the *Occupational Outlook Handbook,* and academic databases including *Academic Search Complete, CareerOneStop* and *ProQuest Career & Technical Education*. We directed students to seek a variety of sources, not only Googled web sites.

Outcome Anthology

Gaby consolidated all of the final career dream essays into a digitized anthology (image below), and then shared it with the class. We were pleased with this demonstration of the students' proficiency in using quality information sources, and with the level of their introspection while reflecting on future career paths.

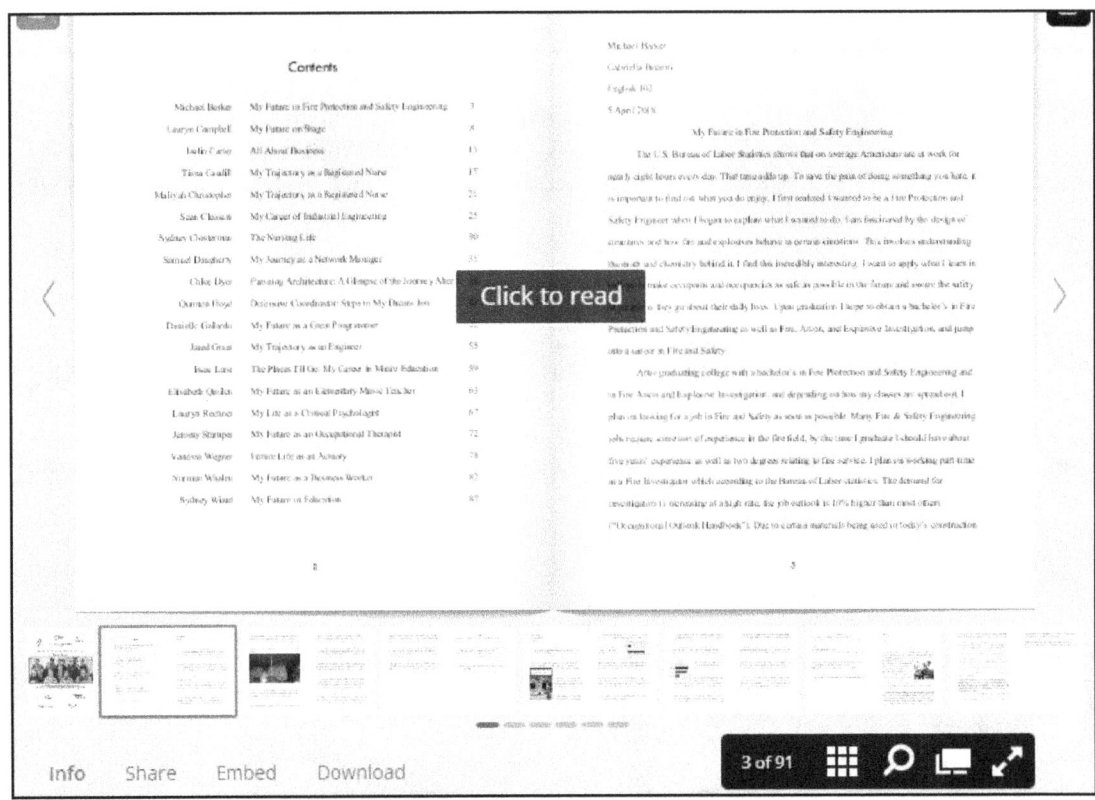

Figure 3: Digitized Flip Book Version of Anthology

The Students' Reflections

On the Course Evaluations, more than 85% of the respondents identified Essay 3 as the most valuable assignment of the semester because it required they think about their career plans:

What particular assignment did you find valuable this semester and why?
1. The last essay because it let me plan for my future.
2. I enjoyed the two papers discussing my career because it made me validate why I wanted to be an architect.
3. The last essay, made me think about my future.
4. The final essay I found enjoyable because it let us look into the future and think about what we want to do with ourselves.
5. The 3rd essay, made us think outside the box.
6. Essay 3—made me think long term.
7. 3rd essay talked of our future
8. Our third essay was a little bit of a struggle but I felt like it was the most valued paper.
9. I enjoyed writting [sic] and researching my future career.
10. Essay 3 because I'm learning new ways of thinking that I can definitately [sic] use in the future.

More than a third of the respondents specified learning how to research:

What are two or three important things you learned in this course?
1. Using credible sources
2. I have learned how to better utilize sources.
3. How to find relevant information, how many sources are appropriate
4. Sources
5. How to properly use databases

Karen and Gaby's Reflections

Contrary to expectation that my Generation Z first-year students lived too much in the moment to think critically about their future, reading their anthology, taught Gaby otherwise. As one student wrote, "the choices we make now will determine our futures." Nine of the twenty essays used the word "excited" in their conclusions, as in "I am incredibly excited to begin my journey" and "When I think about my life, I get excited over all my professional goals that I want to achieve." We hope what they wrote in *What Do You Want to Be When You Grow Up: Career Dreams* will help the writers maintain the momentum for their journeys.

Gaby Bedetti, Eastern Kentucky University
Karen Gilbert, Eastern Kentucky University

Constructing Images and Essential Questions that Critically Respond to a Theme

How can students from various majors incorporate critical thinking through themes and image-making into their lives in meaningful ways, increasing their media literacy and ability to make connections between disciplines? How can an image represent a student's understanding of a theme or issue? What tools need to be provided to students to guide this form of interpretation and image production?

Introduction to Art Education (ART 195) is a course open to students from across the university that counts for creative arts credit, as part of liberal education requirements for graduation. One of the major course objectives is to explore how artists respond to themes and big ideas through their artwork to create meaning and to relate that process to teaching art and developing curriculum. The learning outcome associated with the objective is to create a series of personal artwork based on a theme and develop a comprehensive standards-based lesson plan.

To assist students in distinguishing between themes and subject matter of an image (Walker, 2001), we explore contemporary art and discuss Duncum's (2013) elements of realistic-style pictures. We look at examples of images representing different approaches to constructing images, including angles of view, framing, lighting, depth of field and body language. We discuss how the approach changes the meaning or the mood for the viewer and how the artist has the power to impact meaning by his or her choices when constructing the image.

Much of contemporary art is unfamiliar and sometimes uncomfortable to students, providing a platform for critical analysis. Additionally, since the artists we discuss are living, there is access to first-hand interviews with them about their work. We can hear directly from the artist about the work, rather than relying on second-hand accounts.

Contemporary art is representative of issues relevant in the world today, and artists themselves represent that diversity. The themes and issues that inspire contemporary artists can connect to all disciplines and can be examined through lenses of those subject areas. Students must think critically to make these connections.

First, I show students an image of Janine Antoni's *Gnaw* (1992), which consists of an installation of two 600-pound cubes, one of chocolate and one of lard, and by-products: lipsticks and heart-shaped packaging, in the context of an art museum gallery setting. We discuss what they notice and questions they have as they look closer at the image, one at a time; we build upon their observations and co-constructed knowledge. Then I give each student a wrapped piece of chocolate and ask them to think about sensory aspects of eating the chocolate and memories it may evoke from their past experiences. Following that, students read a short excerpt from the artist about the work (2001) and identify themes. Students then watch a segment of the Art21 video (2003) about another one of Antoni's artwork series, *Lick and Lather* (1993), where she uses the same media of chocolate and lard.

With this background, we write essential questions and discuss how they can be significant for exploring themes and big ideas through any subject area. Essential questions should be open-ended and broad. They could be asked at the beginning of a lesson to gauge students' prior understandings and again at the end of a lesson, after a learning experience has taken place. Some examples of essential questions associated with food as a big idea could be: Where does our food come from? What are benefits to buying food locally? How can food be connected to relationships between people? Why do cultures value particular foods? Questions such as these can provoke inquiry-based learning and student-centered learning.

Students are asked to construct an image that incorporates food as the subject matter and as a theme or big idea. They elaborate on their critical thought through the title they provide and written reflection about their image. They consider Duncum's (2013) elements of realistic pictures when constructing their images. I upload all student images on a class webpage, and we look through them one by one as a class, projected large on the screen. The only information we have is the image and the title. Students are asked to guess the theme or big idea that the student artist is communicating. They are asked what they see and what they think it means. Then we ask the artist if we guessed correctly. Students are often surprised by how their image can communicate various meanings, depending on the perspective of the viewer. They gain insight about one another's values through choices made in constructing the images and have opportunity to communicate visually, verbally, and in written form about an idea.

This activity sets students up for success in creating their own artwork series of six images over the semester based on a theme that is significant to them. Students self-design and problem-solve by determining 3 limitations to guide consistency among all their images and by writing a rationale for why their theme is significant to them and how it could connect to others. I find that the practice image students construct based on food (and themes it can elicit) aids students in becoming more critical when discussing images. They aim to associate deeper meaning within images and communicate moments of significance from their lives to others through creating new images and reflections. This skill can be used throughout life and complement any career path; it documents the journey of life and coming to new understandings.

References

Antoni, J. (1992). Gnaw. Retrieved from http://www.janineantoni.net/gnaw/

Antoni, J. (1993). Lick and Lather. Retrieved from http://www.janineantoni.net/lick-and-lather/

Art21. (2003). Janine Antoni in "Loss and Desire". Retrieved from https://art21.org/watch/art-in-the-twenty-first-century/s2/janine-antoni-in-loss-desire-segment/

Museum of Modern Art. (2001). Audio program excerpt Janine Antoni, *MoMA2000: Open Ends (1960–2000)*, September 28, 2000–March 4, 2001.

Duncum, P. (2013). Teaching the elements of realistic-style pictures. *Art Education, 66*(1), 46-51.

Walker, S. R. (2001). *Teaching meaning in artmaking*. Worcester, MA: Davis.

Stephanie Danker, Miami University

Finding Relevancy in the News

Six years ago, I started teaching a college course titled "Computers and Society" that focuses on the relationship between computers, the Internet, and the laws regulating them. I found a great book to serve as a text for the course. Over time, some of its examples became dated because of the fast pace of technology, but it was still better than anything else I could find. Most students find it to be an easy-to-read, engaging book. Additionally, the book is fairly inexpensive, and the authors provide pdf files of all of the book's chapters freely available online. Because of these benefits, I continue to use the book today. Even though the examples are well over a decade old, they are still relevant. To address the lack of example currency, I started having students search for recent news articles, so they could realize the issues we were discussing from the book are still relevant today.

Originally, I simply asked students to find an article related to the topic we were discussing and submit a very brief report to me about it. After doing this for a semester,

I realized the student and I were benefitting from the article, but no one else was benefitting from what anyone else found. An opportunity was being wasted. After a couple of iterations, I arrived at what I now call my "In the News" assignment.

The students know I expect them to read the book before coming to class so they will be prepared to fully participate in the discussion. The In the News assignment reinforces the need to read the chapter, since its submission is due before class when we start a new chapter. To find a related article and write their review, students have to have some idea of what the chapter is about, and what the authors had to say about it.

The In the News assignment is repeated for each chapter and consists of three steps. First, the student searches for a recent (within eighteen months) article that relates to the chapter. This step requires the student to consider the various topics presented in the book and find recent news coverage that relates to any of those topics. This requirement encourages their reading of the chapter and also makes them think about what topics were discussed. Very often students find articles that are only days or weeks old.

Next, once they have found a suitable article, students have a bit of critical thinking and writing to do. The specifications for the written submission are as follows.

1. Create a document that contains all of the following for the article:
2. The title of the article (a few words)
3. A concise description of the article (a sentence or two)
4. A URL for the article (it must be available publicly, i.e. no subscription/membership needed)
5. The page number (or page number range) in our book to which the article most relates.
6. In 150-200 words describe why you selected this item. How does it connect to our book? Does it agree or disagree with the information presented in our book? What about it interests you?

This report is submitted to our learning management system (LMS) for my review and grading. To address specifications 2, 4, and 5, students must critically think about the book chapter and the article, looking for similarities and differences, and comparing both to their understanding of the topic. Students can apply their knowledge when determining what should be in the concise description. They must justify how the article connects to the book, and if it agrees or disagrees with its content, again requiring the application of knowledge. Requiring the book page number helps assure they've read the chapter and understood its content. Thus, by the time they submit their report, students very likely have done a fair amount of critical thinking about at least one topic from the chapter. This process prepares them for sharing and discussion in class.

Lastly, students are required to briefly describe their article in small group discussions in class. Sharing in class is where the rest of the benefit of the In the News assignment occurs. Knowing that some students will not willingly talk to the whole class, I have the class split up into groups of three to five students. Each student in the small group is allowed one minute to describe their article's topic. After each student has shared, the small group has to decide which article is the most interesting. This decision usually leads to further discussion and questions. I allow about ten minutes for this whole process to transpire. At the end of the time, someone from each small group has to deliver to the class a ninety-second to two-minute presentation about the selected article. It usually is delivered by the person who found the article, but I do not require that.

Initially, articles are shared in the small groups. Then, each group's chosen article gets the attention of the full class. As the groups present their chosen articles, I capture a key word or phrase and write them on the board. After all groups have presented, I lead a discussion about the key words and phrases I've collected, asking if there are any common themes or connections amongst them, thus encouraging a bit more critical thinking by putting their knowledge to use. Great discussions sometimes transpire at this point, but even if they don't, a wide-ranging set of articles has been discussed in the classroom in a relatively short period of time. Ultimately, I create a document with the title and URL of each submitted article and post it in the LMS so students can read someone else's article if they found it interesting.

Most students enjoy the In the News assignments, as it allows them to research and discuss something that interests them and is (at least marginally) related to our course. A bit of freedom goes a long way to keep students engaged in class, and importantly, thinking critically.

David L. Largent, Ball State University

Relating Reader's Experiences to Themes from an Assigned Textbook

The use of First-Year Seminar courses is highly encouraged as a method for students to explore critical inquiry and work collaboratively on assigned projects (Kuh, 2008). It is common for such courses to have a required textbook (Ferguson, 2006). The challenge that I find is how to relate themes introduced within the assigned textbook to experiences shared by current students. One solution is to have students photograph their surroundings that depict specific themes presented in the textbook. This teaching technique incorporates the concepts of student gathering and evaluating information and placing it within a context that is familiar.

Textbook Introduction

For this example, the textbook selected for the First-Year Seminar is titled *The Other Wes Moore: One Name, Two Fates* by Wes Moore. To introduce the text I present a short video that promotes the book and introduce several of the characters and themes presented. Some of the themes discussed are family, urban and suburban living, education, drug culture, and violence. I intentionally do not go into detail on the themes as I wish for the students to read and develop their own impressions about the textbook.

Reading and Essay Tests

To gauge reading progress and understanding, three in-class essay tests are administered. The questions require students to provide specific examples from the textbook that demonstrate their knowledge. After each text is graded and returned, a short discussion is conducted to clarify the concepts presented in the book and to help students to relate the fates of the main characters to their current experiences.

The final test asks two questions. One is a fact-based question from the textbook and the second is designed for students to connect their personal experience to one of the themes presented within the book. An example is:

> "… Both of us had second chances…" is a quote found on page 67 of the text. Provide an example from your personal experience that illustrates a time when you were given a second chance. Include details of the situation and the outcome.

This second question sets the stage for the photograph assignment.

Photograph Assignment

The practice of critical thinking skills is the underlining principle for the design of this assignment. Students are paired (or they may self-select) into teams. The assignment (Appendix 1) is distributed to the students after the final test has been returned and discussed. Students are asked to select two themes from a predetermined list. Next, students are to photograph examples from their current surroundings that depict the themes. As many as five images may be used to illustrate one theme. Students are to work together in selecting the themes, identifying photographic images, and presenting their assignment results in class to fellow students. The goal is for students to relate their current environment to circumstances and locations referred to in the textbook.

Students are graded based on their team collaboration, photographs, and explanation or link of their current surroundings to the theme.

Learning Outcomes

Several outcomes identified by Kuh (2008) as necessary for a successful first-year experience course are found in this assignment. First, critical thinking skills are used as students determine how to relate their surroundings to specific themes in the book. This activity helps students to analyze their own environment within the context of the main characters' experiences. Second, the essay tests meet the suggestion that writing skills be incorporated within the course assignments. Finally, cooperatively learning is achieved by having the students work in teams to select the themes, determine the photographs, and present the finding in class.

References

Ferguson, M. (2006). Creating common ground: Common reading and the first year of college. *Peer Review*, *8*(3), 8-10.

Kuh, G. D. (2008). *High-impact educational practices: What they are, who has access to them, and why they matter*. Washington, DC: Association of American Colleges and Universities.

Student Success Seminar | Fall

Group Photograph Project: Relating Current Surroundings to Examples Found in the Textbook

This assignment is designed for students to identify and present two (2) examples from your current surroundings of actual accounts (themes) described in the text *The Other Wes Moore*. The current surroundings must be depicted in photographs taken by the student and presented in class on the assigned due date. Specific details for the assignment are:

1. Photos should be presented in PDF format
2. Up to five (5) photographs may be used to depict one theme
3. Photos and student explanation should relate to an identified theme from the book

Some Themes Found in the Textbook
1. Addiction
2. Domestic Violence
3. Drug Culture
4. Education
5. Family
6. Immigration – melting pot
7. International Travel – 'Study Abroad'
8. Second Chances
9. Single Parent (head-of-household)
10. Suburban v. Urban Living

Robert A. Meyer, University of Cincinnati–Blue Ash College

Inquiry-Based Problem Solving via Online Discussion Boards

In my content-heavy "Introduction to Pharmacology" course, a prerequisite for my institution's Nursing Program, there are many topics that students historically find confusing, frustrating, and challenging, especially since they have little if any previous experience or related knowledge to draw upon. The additional challenge of a 100% online delivery format can be stressful for students at times. The format may be overwhelming even for those who are not new to distance learning (DL). In DL classes, students are expected to successfully navigate the learning platform (Blackboard) and complete all readings, assignments, quizzes, and research projects, thereby demonstrating themselves to be self-regulated and self-motivated learners. Strategic organization of the learning materials and clear descriptions of assignments and expectations are helpful in minimizing the challenges of DL, but, unfortunately, the lack of face-to-face interaction sometimes contributes to the perception of isolation and helplessness. (Croft, Dalton, & Grant, 2010). In my experience, one-on-one intervention with students to help them comprehend and apply challenging content is not always practical in online courses, nor is it necessarily effective in helping foster students' development as self-regulated and critically thinking learners. Metacognitive activities have been shown to have a beneficial influence on developing critical thinking (Magno, 2010). In addition, a positive correlation between metacognition and self-regulated learning exists (Zimmerman, 1990).

Recently I developed this simple innovation to my course, a self-driven discussion board inquiry activity, to utilize students' analysis of their own thought process to help them mature as critical thinkers by overcoming the obstacle of a personally perplexing concept.

I introduced this assignment during week two of the semester while covering the many fundamental concepts related to how drugs are absorbed, distributed, metabolized, and excreted by the body. Students were asked to choose a topic they found especially baffling, outline exactly what their difficulty was, and specifically show how they were able to overcome this challenge by deeper investigation. The emphasis was on describing their process and sharing any helpful links or resources. The assignment for this unit was posted on Blackboard with clear instructions of expectations. Students were also asked to submit a substantive response to another student's post on their own challenging topic, citing additional helpful resources and adding their own comments and clarifications on the topic. Instructions on the Discussion Board are given below.

> The purpose of this and similar assignments is to provide an opportunity for application of the material you have learned regarding general pharmacological principles.
>
> Part 1: Choose a topic from Unit 2 which was somewhat confusing to you initially, and which you investigated by using your textbook and/or the web, helping you gain a clearer understanding. Go to the Discussion Board and click on Unit 2 Assignment. Click on Create Thread. Write 2-3 paragraphs of at least 5 sentences each summarizing the challenging concept and your area of confusion and describe in detail precisely how your investigation clarified this for you. Include the textbook page and any website links that proved helpful in your inquiry.
>
> Part 2: Read several other students' posts and respond to one student post in a substantive manner, either sharing additional references or clarifying an area of confusion related to a concept using evidence from a valid source. Bring something useful to the table; don't just say "Great job!" or "I agree!" No fluff permitted, just real substance citing reliable scientific references.

As educators, we know that frustration, though uncomfortable, can be highly motivating for us, and also, in theory, for our students. I employed this emotion to help fuel the process of self-driven inquiry to solve an immediate problem and to help students to view their own explorative process as a tool for dealing with future course content and for future academic and professional hurdles. Students wrote about their conundrums, shared newly-discovered resources with one another, and had extensive, lively interchanges on the discussion board. Many, if not most, students responded more often than was required, thanking each other for the helpful tips and relating that their understanding increased considerably afterwards, allowing them to break through their own learning barrier and get "unstuck." This activity also supported deeper learning of difficult concepts, as students had their eyes opened to new perspectives and discovered that they were gaining deeper comprehension and insight with each additional student response. In future iterations of this assignment, I will ask students to complete some feedback questions, but for this round, the positive student-to-student interaction indicated that it proved beneficial and provoked a desire for further inquiry into their topics. It also laid the foundation for discussion board assignments in future weeks in which students read and responded to other students' research papers, following their own question-trail and probing deeper, making connections and seeking clarification. It was encouraging to see that they became more adept at scientific investigation using reliable sources.

References

Magno, C. (2010). The role of metacognitive skills in developing critical thinking. *Metacognition and Learning, 5*, 137-156. doi.org/10.1007/s11409-010-9054-4

Croft, N., Dalton, A. & Grant, M. (2010). Overcoming isolation in distance learning: Building a learning community through time and space. *Journal for Education in the Built Environment, 5*(1). 27-64.

Zimmerman, B.J. (1990). Self-regulated learning and academic achievement: An overview. *Educational Psychologist, 25*(1), 3-17, doi: 10.1207/s15326985ep2501_2

Ann R. Witham, University of Cincinnati—Blue Ash College

Debating as Critical Thinking

In our days of teaching two sections of either ENG 101 or 102 per semester, we were always trying to create assignments that both met the course's objectives and were interesting. As the course contained both oral and written objectives, one of our favorite critical thinking exercises was an informal debate.

Since we both taught at the same time and the same first-year courses, it was easy to combine our class into a debate. After semesters of trying to find a topic that would interest our students, we settled on Resolved: Kentucky should legalize marijuana. While today 33 states have legalized pot, it wasn't until 1996 that California, of course, led the way. Unlike with controversies such as the fair tax, flat tax, or farm subsidies, students had skin in the game as each year studies showed more and more of them were sampling weed.

To set up the debate, one class was chosen to be the pro side and one the anti. We served as judges, and in the beginning we found it helpful for our students and us to choose the issues—usually the physical effects, the psychological effects, and the financial side. Classes were broken into team to research and present the issues. Each side got around six minutes to present each issue. On the Debate Day, one of us brought his class over to the opposition's classroom.

Unlike traditional debate, we kept the structure loose, and we never declared a winner. Students were encouraged to take notes because the material in the debate became the evidence they could use in their subsequent themes on the subject.

Critical thinking slipped silently into their papers. To ensure their best reasoning powers, the next paper we had them write was always the counter argument for the side they took during debate week. Not surprisingly, this reversed point of view provided a large degree of difficulty for most students.

In retrospect, the two related assignments taught a lot, but what stands out today was the critical thinking standard of **Perspective**. It's much easier to research, present orally, and write up something that you fervently believe. What's hard is taking the opposing point of view, walking the proverbial mile in another person's shoes.

Charlie Sweet, Eastern Kentucky University
Hal Blythe, Eastern Kentucky University

Role Plays: Sometime Awkward, But Very Often Effective

Groans are typically audible across the classroom after we announce an upcoming role play. Role plays can be awkward and anxiety provoking. As uncomfortable as they may be, research suggests a positive relationship between role plays and critical thinking (Abrami, Bernard, Borokhovski, Waddington, Wade, &Persson, 2015; Eunsook, 2018).

According to Abrami et al. (2015), critical thinking is "purposeful, self-regulatory judgment that results in interpretation, analysis, evaluation, and inference, as well as explanations of the considerations on which that judgment is based" (p. 275). In order to promote critical thinking, we must present situations with situations that foster analysis and problem-solving skills. Role plays are the perfect opportunity to present students with problems that are applicable to real-life situations in order to encourage them to think critically.

Researchers dating back to 1907 criticized rote learning, suggesting learning should occur in the context of a problem that appeared relevant to the student. Authentic/anchored instruction provides a well-defined, real-world problem for students to consider. Role playing requires students to analyze a relevant problem and react accordingly, in a simulated situation. As such, role playing has been found to hold an important role in promoting critical thinking skills (Abrami et al., 2015).

Eunsook (2018) recently conducted a study in which nursing students engaged in a simulation exercise after either receiving a lecture on the topic or participating in a role play. The results of the study indicated having the role play prior to the simulation exercise was a more effective teaching technique than to have a lecture prior to the simulation exercise. Further, the role play led to an improvement in self-efficacy and critical thinking skills of the nursing students, as well as to a deeper understanding of clinical situations.

So how can we make role plays less intimidating and awkward for students? Any project or activity that involves the entire class watching a small group of students is likely to increase the anxiety of those being watched. Thus, I have found that conducting several role plays at once in smaller groups of students feels less intimidating, allowing students to think through their responses without the additional pressure of a classroom of eyes on them. Additionally, it is important for students and professors to mutually agree on a set of rules or boundaries to put in place during role plays and simulations. For example, training peers to provide feedback in a constructive, as opposed to critical, manner can help minimize the fear of making mistakes. Establishing these guidelines for role plays encourages students to be willing to improve their critical thinking skills through practicing the often messy, complex, real-life situations they will encounter in their professional lives.

References

Abrami, P. C., Bernard, R. M., Borokhovski, E., Waddington, D. I., Wade, C. E., & Persson, T. (2015). Strategies for teaching students to think critically: A meta-analysis. *Review of Educational Research, 85*(2). 275-314. doi: 10.3102/0034654314551063

Eunsook, K. (2018). Effect of simulation-based emergency cardiac arrest education on nursing students' self-efficacy and critical thinking skills: Roleplay versus lecture. *Nurse Education Today, 61*, 258-263. doi.org/10.1016/j.nedt.2017.12.003

Anna Grace Cooper, Spalding University
Nathanael G. Mitchell, Spalding University
Robin Morgan, Indiana University Southeast

Building Students' Critical Thinking Skills in One Minute: Effort and Engagement Questions

Introduction

Incorporating creative teaching strategies into the classroom increases students' interest in content and results in higher levels of critical thinking and student learning (Harrington & Zakrajsek, 2017; Saphier et al., 2014). Because rewarding student effort can result in high levels of motivation and a growth mindset (Dweck, 2006), educators should find ways to encourage student effort, instead of primarily emphasizing exam scores when determining student grades. Our one-minute Effort and Engagement (E&E) teaching activity accomplishes the goals of critical thinking development, student engagement, and rewarding student effort in a creative, effective way. It is easy to apply to any discipline.

One-Minute Effort and Engagement Teaching Activity

At the end of most class meetings, we distribute a piece of paper to each student and then display an **"Effort and Engagement" (E&E) question**, which students have 1 minute to answer on a piece of paper they turn in. Our E&E questions correspond to multiple levels of Bloom and Krathwohl's (1956) desired educational outcomes within the cognitive domain. We use a variety of questions (see Appendix A) that require critical thinking skills, including checking for content understanding, applying content to one's life, sharing opinions on controversial topics, and using content to achieve greater self-awareness. We review students' responses and spend the first minute of our next class sharing them. In addition to critical thinking development, this activity is designed to encourage effort and engagement; therefore, students receive one point for each response, even if their responses are "wrong" (e.g., the example given is a positive correlation, but the student writes that it's negative).

Effectiveness of E&E Questions

To gauge the effectiveness of our E&E questions, students completed a 6-item, anonymous questionnaire assessing the E&E activity, with space for open-ended comments, at the end of the course. Each item was rated between 1 (strongly disagree) and 5 (strongly agree). The responses are below.

Survey Responses

Item	Mean	SD
1) I thought the E&E questions were interesting to answer.	4.68	.51
2) I appreciated the chance to earn up to 25/25 points by answering E&E questions.	4.91	.29
3) The E&E questions helped solidify relevant course material.	4.59	.67
4) Hearing the results of the E&E questions often provided insight into my peers' thoughts.	4.70	.48
5) Overall, I liked the E&E point questions part of our class.	4.71	.50
6) I think you should keep the E&E point questions for future sections of this class.	4.85	.35

N = 202 undergraduates.

Open-Ended Responses: Many of the students made comments on their questionnaires. No negative comments were received. Examples of their comments are:
- The E&E questions made me think carefully about what we just learned.
- Great way to connect material to my life personally and the real world in general.
- E&E questions challenged us to think outside the box, on our own, not just let others think for us.
- Questions kept me engaged and provided real world insight.
- E&E questions really made me think about my opinions, which I loved.
- I loved learning my peers' opinions and discovering how different [our opinions] sometimes were.
- For as long as you teach, these questions should remain.

Results confirm E&E questions increase critical thinking, content understanding, effort, and engagement. Utilizing our E&E teaching technique provides many benefits for educators and students:
- Rice (2018) states that closing pauses may be the *most* powerful teaching tool at our disposal but are often forgotten or neglected. E&E questions are placed strategically at the end of each class meeting so students leave having just utilized critical thinking skills in answering the questions.

- Content is reviewed at the beginning of the following class, further reinforcing content.
- Students' self-esteem and motivation can increase through early successes (McGuire & McGuire, 2015); our E&E activity allows students to earn an E&E point the first day of class!
- Educators can learn about their students' thoughts & beliefs and assess content comprehension.
- Students are grateful for a fun, engaging technique that helps solidify course material.

Appendix A: Types and Examples of E&E Questions

Type	Example
Checking for content understanding	Would you expect # of hours spent brushing your teeth and # of cavities at your next dental exam to be positively or negatively correlated?
Applying content to one's life	What are 2 groups or people off which you currently BIRG (bask in the reflected glory)?
Sharing opinions on controversial topics	Which best captures your opinion of the death penalty? Give a reason why. a) I support it. b) I oppose it. c) I support it, but only in certain cases.
Applying information to the future	Given our discussion of rates of violence in the school system, do you think rates will increase or decrease over the next 10 years? Give a reason why.
Using content to achieve greater self-awareness	What strategy discussed today can you try to reduce your own procrastination?

References

Bloom, B.S., & Krathwohl, D.R. (1956). *Taxonomy of educational objectives: The classification of educational goals, by a committee of college and university examiners.* New York, NY: Longmans.

Dweck, C. (2006). *Mindset: The new psychology of success.* New York, NY: Ballantine.

Harrington, C., & Zakrajsek, T. (2017). *Dynamic lecturing: Research-based strategies to enhance lecture effectiveness.* Sterling, VA: Stylus.

McGuire, S.Y., & McGuire, S. (2015). *Teach students how to learn.* Sterling, VA: Stylus.

Rice, G.T. (2018). *Hitting pause: 65 lecture breaks to refresh and reinforce learning.* Sterling, VA: Stylus.

Saphier, J., Haley-Speca, M.A., & Gower, R. (2008). *The skillful teacher: Building your teaching skills* (6th ed.). Acton, MA: Research for Better Teaching, Inc.

Karyn McKenzie, Georgetown College
Lisa Eddy, Ed.D., Georgetown College

Interactive Participatory Class Activities that Stimulate Critical Thinking

Critical thinking is not a gift that students are born with; rather, most of them have to work to acquire this skill. I have found that critical thinking can be cultivated in a classroom setting by engaging students in interactive, participatory small group activities—often referred to as the Collaborative Learning (CL) design. The CL philosophy of teaching, in short, uses an interactive, participatory learning method to encourage students to work and learn together in in small groups in order to acquire knowledge relative to the course content (Gokhale, 1995). The CL method can motivate students to analyze, evaluate, and synthesize course materials and content, which ultimately helps to bolster their critical thinking skills.

I support the definition of critical thinking devised by the National Council for Excellence in Critical Thinking (NCECT, 1987): "Critical thinking is the intellectually disciplined process of actively and skillfully conceptualizing, applying, analyzing, synthesizing, and/or evaluating information gathered from, or generated by, observation, experience, reflection, reasoning, or communication, as a guide to belief and action." To encourage students to use critical thinking skills, I engage them in the following activities: role-play, debates, participatory learning activities, multi-media supplemental aids, and Internet technology. These tools help to stimulate learning by promoting open discussions and focused dialectics.

Because I teach leadership courses in the College of Education, I am always looking for strategies to teach complicated subject matter in a way that students will appreciate and understand. My teaching methods entail challenging students to not only investigate and explore the subject matter seriously, but also to uncover ways to apply it to everyday situations. One technique I use to promote this objective is to bring corrugated paper masks and paint to class; with these materials, I encourage students to design a mask that depicts themselves as leaders. After the masks have been painted, the students openly share the meaning of their particular design with their peers. The exercise is not only reflective and thought-provoking, but also fun and self-revealing. Students are often surprised by what their mask designs reveal about themselves. In addition, I debrief the students by sharing authentic stories and media about successful leaders, as well as integrating writing assignments that require students to make the connection between famous leaders and themselves.

Another CL-style practice that I often utilize to boost students' understanding of the course material is an exercise involving boxes of tinker toys™. Coff and Hatfield (2003) argue that this exercise can be very valuable for teaching strategic management skills, and I have also found that it can help students better understand the critical thinking process. The purpose of the exercise is to encourage students to solve difficult problems by developing team-building and leadership skills. Students are randomly assigned to small teams and have to work together to build a sturdy structure. I give each group 30 minutes to build their structure; at the end of the time limit, the group with the sturdiest structure wins. Each group is then required to complete a short questionnaire about their experience. Afterwards, students engage in a group discussion, and I share the key learning goals of the exercise.

As another CL technique, I have brought cartons of eggs to class to illustrate how students can walk on the eggs without breaking them. I tell them that the process of walking on eggs is one that literally requires exceptional caution, incredible skill, and a sense of self-control that would be nothing short of amazing (Steve Spangler Science, 2018). I use this exercise to demonstrate how delicate communication is when working in organizations. Students are always captivated by seeing if someone in class can actually walk on eggs without breaking them. Usually, one student will manage to do it, at which point I debrief the class on the essential relationship between communication and leadership. I share with the class that although communications is a delicate process, just like walking on eggs, it can be accomplished with careful planning and attention to detail.

Through all these exercises, I encourage students in my classes to engage in active debates in order to better understand all sides of a particular topic. The exercise that I most employ in this regard is the Oxford Style Debate. This debate style gives students an opportunity to argue for or against a particular topic. Students work in teams and spend time outside of the classroom collecting data to support their argument. After finalizing their data collection, the students return to class for the debate. The Oxford Style Debate has been a very successful technique in motivating students to explore and research a topic before debating it in class. I have noticed that the students enjoy the competitive debate format, and thus they work diligently to find the most convincing information to prove that their side of the debate is the best alternative. As a critical thinking teaching method, the Oxford Style Debate offers a research-based practice that identifies factual information.

The tips that I described have worked for me and provide excellent critical thinking exercises that enhance students' learning outcomes.

References

Coff, R. W., & Hatfield, D. E. (2003). Tinkering in class: Using the Tinker Toy exercise to teach first mover advantages and the resource-based view. *Journal of Strategic Management Education, 1*(1), 1-15.

Gokhale, A. A. (1995). Collaborative learning enhances critical thinking. *Journal of Technology Education, 7*(1).

Steve Spangler Science. (2018). *Walking on eggshells.* Retrieved from https://www.stevespanglerscience.com/lab/experiments/walking-on-eggshells/

Sherwood Thompson, Eastern Kentucky University

Forcing Students to Make an Informed Choice

A few years ago, I had the opportunity and desire to have students in one of my courses consider the lack of diversity in our major (computer science) and what implications that might have on the profession and society in general. I added a variety of mini-lectures, activities, and assignments to the course focused on diversity and inclusivity designed to make them more aware of the issue. One assignment in particular, required the students to write an essay where they had to do a bit of research, make an informed choice between scenarios, and justify their choice. Although my application was making students more aware of diversity and inclusivity issues in computer science, I believe this assignment could be adapted to most any domain and topic.

I titled the assignment "Diversity Position Paper–Working in a group to produce a presentation and paper" and provided the students with the following overview.

> You are to research, reflect, and then write about diversity in relation to working in a group to produce a presentation and related paper. Meet the basic specifications, think deeply, and give it your best thought. That said, if you don't push yourself, that's on you and you're wasting your time and money here. To complete this essay successfully, you must successfully complete all specifications, which I have listed below.

The intent of this essay is to have you consider three possible compositions of a group tasked with developing a presentation and associated paper, and then take a stance in favor of one of them, providing advantages and disadvantages, and appropriate documentation to substantiate your chosen group composition. This should also prepare you to have a thoughtful conversation about course content.

I then provided the follow description for the essay they were to research and write.

Read the three possible group compositions, each with a brief justification (provided below in the Scenario section). Consider which group composition most closely aligns with your beliefs and current understanding. Compose an essay which states and justifies your choice. Your essay should be no shorter than 750 words and no longer than 1000.

Scenario: *Imagine you are going to be one of three or four members of a group tasked with developing a paper and presentation on a particular subject in a relatively short period of time. Which of the following three options will you use to select the other members of your group?*

1. **The group should consist of only subject matter experts.** *Since you have a limited amount of time to develop and refine your paper and presentation, you want to have as much expertise as possible at your disposal, and thus want the entire group to be subject matter experts.*
2. **The group should be diverse, including subject matter experts, as well as others.** *Since you have a limited amount of time to develop and refine your paper and presentation, you want subject matter experts, but also want others who can offer differing points of view.*
3. **It does not matter if the group is diverse or all subject matter experts, as long as there is at least one subject matter expert.** *Since you have a limited amount of time to develop and refine your paper and presentation, you want a group of individuals who will work together, and do not care if they are subject matter experts or not, as long as someone has knowledge of the subject.*

The detailed specifications for the assignment included the following.

The essay must contain the following sections:
1. **Introduction:** *Describe the group composition you have chosen and provide a very brief summary of why you have chosen it.*

2. ***Support***: *Provide brief summaries of at least two reliable articles, papers, or books which lend support for your chosen group composition.*
3. ***Advantages:*** *Discuss the advantages of using the group composition you have chosen.*
4. ***Disadvantages:*** *Discuss the disadvantages of using the group composition you have chosen.*
5. ***Comparison:*** *Compare the three group compositions and describe why you feel your chosen composition is better than the other two group compositions.*
6. ***Closing:*** *Summarize your position and why you have selected it.*
7. *The essay must utilize **appropriate citations**. You may choose the citation style.*

Students tend to read the three scenarios, have a favorite, and jump into writing their essays. Then they get to the part where they have to justify their choice, including citing articles that support their choice, and that activity slows them down a bit. Many times, students have told me that they made an immediate choice from the scenarios, but then changed their mind after researching articles to find support for their original choice. Not only did they struggle to find support for their original choice, they found convincing support for another choice.

Occasionally, students will get creative. They decide they don't like any of the scenarios I provide and create their own. Sometimes it is a completely new scenario, and sometimes simply a slight modification of one of the three I provided. As long as the student provides adequate support for their choice, I award credit.

This assignment asks students to use their knowledge and apply it in their decision-making process as they make an informed choice between the three scenarios. They must critically think about the implications of the three group compositions and compare that to their past experiences of working with groups to decide what they believe will produce the best results. But I don't just ask them for their opinion; they have to justify and support it with research. Again, they're required to think critically about the articles they find to decide if they support (or not) their chosen scenario. And lastly, the student must identify both advantages and disadvantages of using the group composition they have chosen, along with providing a comparison of the three scenarios and why theirs is best.

David L. Largent, Ball State University

An Effective Practice Tip for Critical Thinking

The High-Impact Practice Addressed: Writing Intensive Courses

"Writing Intensive Courses: The benefits of learning to write well also include the improvement of *critical thinking skills and improvements in students' confidence in their ability to succeed in college courses* (Brownell, et. al., 2013; Kellog & Whiteford, 2012; Bean, 2011; Fulwiler, 1982). In assigning *multiple drafts of compositions* and *offering formative assessments of each draft*, instructors often *help students become more attentive to the quality of their thinking as well as the clarity and logic of their assertions* (Myhill & Jones, 2007; Flower & Hayes, 1981). (Gorzycki, n.d.) Retrieved from https://ctfd.sfsu.edu/content/high-impact-teaching-practices#Common Intellectual Experiences).

The Tip

The class being mentioned teaches health care documentation skills. The students tend to have difficulty being flexible; rather, they write in formulaic patterns. I wanted to help them develop the skill to compose and edit therapy goals in a dynamic fashion, changing and reflecting, changing again, until the goal reads well and says what they intended, rather than getting stuck, or writing in one template pattern for all goals. The following tip has worked to help students integrate the ability to manipulate words and components in order to say what they intend and to have a focused clear meaning.

In class, I type a goal on screen in large readable font. We read the first goal together as a class. The goal used as an example is taken from student work, and the unidentified student has agreed before class for their goal to be used as an example. We then move to the goal right below, which is the same goal written again. Both goals appear simultaneously on screen. Text colors for the second goal are changed as I begin to edit that second version of the goal.

The class is now asked to identify problematic issues in the goal. I mediate my facilitation based on their answers. If the students need more help initially, I will provide more direction. The changes are made on screen in the different color. The facilitation and changing will go on for several minutes until the class and I are satisfied with how the goal reads. We review as a class what is different about the revised version of the goal and which principles were used to make the goal more cohesive. This is a facilitated and teacher-modeled approach.

Next, the class receives a handout with two more goals that need correction. The students practice the same type of revision in small groups. I circulate between the groups, providing direction or questioning their work, as indicated. The process is the same, except that my scaffolding process removes Instructor modeling, but still provides facilitation to the small groups. When finished, the groups reconvene as a class.

The goal worked on in small group format is also written on the screen twice, just as in the beginning of class. The first version of the goal is left untouched. The second time the goal appears on screen, it is modified in a new color, incorporating the small group suggestions. I scaffold further by withholding advice and letting the groups themselves discuss what principles they addressed (ex- changing short term goal words to long term goal words, matching the measures to the types of issues). The groups address each other's comments. Eventually, the class arrives at a final version that is acceptable to the majority of the class. If there is time, the process will be repeated with an additional goal. Finally, the students reflect on what skills they called upon to make the edit, and how they knew the goal was in its final ready stage.

Typically, the class will then have an out- of- class graded assignment that calls upon the skills just applied. I find that instead of lecturing to the students about how to craft a well worded, properly sequenced, targeted goal with clear measures, and logical in intent, it is more effective to involve them in the editing and crafting process with scaffolded mediation. The format of multiple drafts and use of formative assessment of the outcome during several stages not only helps students gain confidence in their expressive abilities, but also in their higher level thinking abilities, especially in the areas of analyzing and evaluating as well as in constructing and creating a revised improved goal (Anderson et al, 2001).

I asked the students if they felt more professional at the end of the semester after having learned this process. They replied that they felt smarter. It seems that they felt an increase in their critical thinking abilities.

References

Anderson, L. W., & Krathwohl, D., et al. (Eds.) (2001). *A taxonomy for learning, teaching, and assessing: A revision of Bloom's taxonomy of educational objectives.* New York, NY: Longman.

Gorzycki, M. (n.d.) *High-impact teaching practices.* Retrieved from https://ctfd.sfsu.edu/content/high-impact-teaching-practices#Common Intellectual Experiences)

Geela Spira, Eastern Kentucky University

Each One Write One

Need a source for your students to analyze for critical thinking and are frustrated because you can't find a good one? Have you considered the possibility of writing it yourself? We did, and it paid off for over thirty years.

Years ago, when we were teaching two sections of ENG 101 or ENG 102 each semester, we included a unit on critical thinking. We were supposed to have the students assess an essay through the prism of the basic elements of critical thinking. Unfortunately, the department kept changing readers. When we allowed the students to choose their own essays, what they discovered were inappropriate, possessed a high degree of difficulty for analysis, or were too esoteric for them or us to understand. In addition, whether an essay in a reader or an article in a magazine/journal, the pieces were too long for the students to review in approximately 500 words.

The ideal piece for analysis needed to be short enough, of general interest to students of all backgrounds and majors, and replete with a variety of critical thinking errors. When we couldn't find our ideal piece, we created it.

"Just One Deadly Drink for the Road" purported to be an editorial from the *Woodhole Gazette* by the paper's editor, Olliver Bradley. The piece was a well-organized call for action in support of the mythical State House Bill 1 that clamped down on drunk drivers. Bradley's editorial contained three major issues, and each issue was supported by three pieces of attributed evidence. In short, Bradley's essay read well.

Over the years, students applied various critical thinking standards (Elder and Paul had yet to invent a systematic approach) that our textbooks trumpeted. Years later, after Elder and Paul had started their Foundation for Critical Thinking and our university had adopted a QEP (Quality Enhancement Plan) on critical and creative thinking, we used the Bradley essay to train faculty as QEP Coaches. Obviously, the faculty were much better at applying standards, especially since by then Elder and Paul had developed their systematic approach (see for instance Paul and Elder's *The Miniature Guide to Critical Thinking: Concepts and Tools*).

Interestingly, whether the Bradley essay was used by students or faculty, the editorial almost always revealed a flaw in critical thinking. Despite our audience employing standards such as **Objectivity**, **Sufficiency**, **Perspective**, **Relevancy**, and **Specificity**, the standard that always seemed to trip them up was **Accuracy**. When we wrote the original editorial, we used nine pieces of evidence, ranging from quotations by experts to studies by various insurance institutes. Like the editorial itself and Olliver Bradley, all nine sources were complete fiction. Not once in all the years we used Bradley's harangue did a single student or faculty member bother to check either the actuality of the

Woodhole Gazette, the validity of any of the nine sources, or even the very existence of the editorialist.

What's the point? Was P. T. Barnum right about suckers? Maybe, but we stressed that to employ critical thinking effectively, one must use ALL the standards. In this age of fake news, checking sources is more important than ever to develop students, faculty, and citizens in general to their highest potential.

Charlie Sweet, Eastern Kentucky University
Hal Blythe, Eastern Kentucky University

Afterword

In the past twenty-one years, we have produced twelve books in the "It Works for Me" series. Hal and Charlie co-edited the first seven, and Russell joined the team for the last five. This past year Hal and Charlie finally retired, so, starting next year, Russell will take over the reins of the series. Hal and Charlie had a great run, but they couldn't have done it without the contributions of so many from across the country. What began as a one-shot blossomed into a full-blown series, thanks mostly to the guidance of our publisher, Doug Dollar, who took a chance on what in 1998 was at the far end of the SOTL spectrum. Hal and Charlie will miss his comments, his suggestions for covers, and even his appearance at an early Pedagogicon on our campus.

For those who like to work ahead, Russell is happy to announce that the 2020 volume in the "It Works for Me" series will be *It Works for Me with iGens*. He is looking for practical tips to help instructors deal with that new generation (Z) appearing on college and university campuses, even if only online. Please address all submissions to russell.carpenter@eku.edu by 5 January 2020, and follow our traditional guidelines. A formal CFP will be sent out in the fall.

About the Authors

Charlie Sweet, Ph.D. (Florida State University, 1970), is the former Co-Director of the Teaching & Learning Center at Eastern Kentucky University. With Hal, he has collaborated on over 1200 published works, including 32 books, literary criticism, educational research, and ghostwriter of the lead novella for the *Mike Shayne Mystery Magazine*.

Hal Blythe, Ph.D. (University of Louisville, 1972), is the former Co-Director of the Teaching & Learning Center at Eastern Kentucky University. With Charlie, he has collaborated on over 1200 published works, including 32 books (twelve in New Forums' popular It Works for Me Series), literary criticism, and educational research.

Russell Carpenter, Ph.D. (University of Central Florida, 2009), directs the Noel Studio for Academic Creativity and Minor in Applied Creative Thinking at Eastern Kentucky University where he is also Assistant Professor of English. He is the author or editor of several recent books including *The Routledge Reader on Writing Centers and New Media* (with Sohui Lee), *Cases on Higher Education Spaces*, *Teaching Applied Creative Thinking* (with Charlie Sweet, Hal Blythe, and Shawn Apostel), and the *Introduction to Applied Creative Thinking* (with Charlie Sweet and Hal Blythe). He serves as President of the Southeastern Writing Center Association and Past Chair of the National Association of Communication Centers.

www.ingramcontent.com/pod-product-compliance
Lightning Source LLC
Chambersburg PA
CBHW080405170426
43193CB00016B/2822